NTA UGC

NET/JRF/SET

GENERAL

PAPER - I

Simranjit kaur and Neha Raghuwanshi

Published By

Invincible Publication Pvt.Ltd.

INVINCIBLE
Publication Private Limited

Published by

Invincible Publication Pvt. Ltd.

1103-A, 11th Floor SAS Tower, Sector 38, Gurugram - 12200

www.invinciblepublishers.com

First Edition 2023

Book Name: NTA UGC NET/JRF/SET General Paper-1

Author: Simranjit kaur and Neha Raghuwanshi

ISBN: 978-81-9639-187-4

Invincible Publication Pvt. Ltd.

Sales Office: 4760-61/23, Basement, Pratap Street, Ansari Road,

Daryaganj, New Delhi- 110002

Email: invinciblepublishers@gmail.com

CONTENTS

CHAPTER 1

TEACHING APTITUDE

Teaching: Concept, objectives, levels of teaching (memory, understanding, and reflective), characteristics, and basic requirements

- Learner's characteristics: Characteristics of adolescent and adult learners (academic, social, emotional, and cognitive), individual differences
- Factors affecting teaching related to: Teacher, Learner, Support material, Instructional facilities, Learning environment, and Institution
- Methods of teaching in institutions of higher learning: Teacher centered vs. learner-centered methods; offline vs. online methods (Swayam, Swayamprabha, MOOCs, etc.)
- Teaching support system: Traditional, modern, and ICT based
- Evaluation systems: Elements and types of evaluation, evaluation in Choice Based Credit System in higher education, computer-based testing, innovations in the evaluation system.

TEACHING

- Teaching is a process in which one individual teaches or instructs another individual.

Teaching is considered the act of imparting instructions to the learners in the classroom situation.

The aims of teaching with respect to its various modes, are as follows:

- Teaching – to bring changes in the behaviour of the student.
- Conditioning – to improve the learning skills of students.
- Training – shaping the behaviour and conduct.
- Instruction – Acquisition of knowledge.
- Indoctrination – Formation of belief.

Characteristics of teaching:-

1. The main character of teaching is to provide guidance and training.
2. Teaching is the interaction between teacher and students.
3. Teaching is the art to give knowledge to students in an effective way.
4. Teaching is a science to educate facts and causes of different topics of different subjects.
5. Teaching is a continuous process.

6. Teacher can teach effectively if he has full confidence in the subject.

7. Teaching encourages students to learn more and more.

8. Teaching is formal as well as informal

9. Teaching is the communication of information to students. In teaching, the teacher imparts information in an interesting way so that students can easily understand the information.

10. Teaching is a tool to help the student to adjust himself in society and its environment.

- **Pedagogy** is the method and practice of teaching. Pedagogy, taken as an academic discipline, is the study of how knowledge and skills are imparted in an educational context, and it considers the interactions that take place during learning. Pedagogy is often described as the act of teaching.
- **Teaching** is all about communication of information, ideas, or skills that can be questioned or discussed, and the facts that are taught in teaching are supported by evidence, whereas **indoctrination** is about communication of beliefs that are not supported by any evidence, and the receiver is supposed to accept it the way it has been taught without any argument or questioning.

Differences

Education	Indoctrination
• Supported by evidence and data. • Encourages the development of people's own beliefs.	• Uses statements or ideas that aren't supported by evidence most of the time • Encourages the acceptance of imposed beliefs

Levels of teaching

- Memory level: Thoughtless teaching
- Understanding level: Thoughtful teaching
- Reflective level: Upper thoughtful level
- Autonomous level

1. Memory level of teaching

It is the first and thoughtless level of teaching. It is concerned with memory or mental ability that exists in all living beings. Teaching at the memory level is considered to be the lowest level of teaching.

Memory Level of Teaching

The Objective Of The Memory Level Of Teaching Is Just To Impart Information Or Knowledge To The Learner

Herbart Is Considered The Exponent Of Memory Level Of Teaching

FEATURES

- The thinking ability does not play any role.
- Students only cram the facts, information, formulas, and laws that are taught to them.
- The teaching is nothing but learning the subject matter by rote or memorizing.
- The role of the teacher is prominent and that of the student is secondary.
- The study material is organized and pre-planned. The teacher presents the study material in sequential order.
- Memory level teaching lacks insight. Psychologically, it is cognitive-level teaching.
- Useful for children in lower classes. This is because their intellect is under development and they have a rote memory.
- The role of the teacher is important in this level of teaching and he/she is free to make choices of subject matter, plan it, and can present it at will.
- The knowledge acquired at memory level teaching forms a basis for the future.
- Memory level teaching acts as the first step for understanding and reflective levels of teaching.
- It is a prerequisite for understanding level teaching.
- This does not contribute to the development of the student's capabilities.
- Since at this level, students learn by rote, the knowledge gained does not prove helpful in real-life situations as it does not develop the talents of students.
- The pupils are kept in strict discipline and cramming is insisted in this teaching.
- Intelligence does not carry any importance in this type of teaching and it lacks motivation.

2. Understanding level

Understanding something is to perceive the meaning, grasp the idea and comprehend the meaning. Given by Morrison.

- seeing the total use of facts
- seeing relationship
- a generalized insight
- The teaching at the understanding level is of a higher quality than the one at the memory level.
- It is more useful and thoughtful from the point of view of mental capabilities. At this level of teaching, the teacher explains the student the relationship between principles and facts and teaches them how these principles can be applied. Memory level teaching barrier is essential to be crossed for this level of teaching.
- At this level of teaching students to make use of their thinking abilities.
- Knowledge acquired at this level forms the basis of the reflective level of teaching.
- Here the teacher presents subject matter before the students in an organized and sequential form. The new knowledge acquired is related to the previously acquired knowledge.
- Here the students do not learn by rote. Here they learn by understanding the facts and information and their use and purpose.
- Teaching at this level is subject centered. There is no interaction between the teacher and students at this level.

3. Reflective level of teaching

- This level is also known as the introspective level. Reflecting on something means giving careful thought to something over a period of time. It also means thinking deeply about something.
- Hunt developed the reflective model.
- Reflective level of teaching is considered to be the highest level at which teaching is carried out.

Reflective Level Of Teaching

- Includes both understanding memory & understanding level teaching.
- The management of teaching at memory & understanding – level taken place before reflective level teaching starts.
- It means " Problem – Centered " teaching.
- Provide opportunities for developing intellectual behaviour.

- It is highly thoughtful and useful.
- A student can attain this level only after going through memory level and understanding level.
- Teaching at the reflective level enables the students to solve the real problems of life. At this level, the student is made to face a real problematic situation. The student by understanding the situation and using his critical abilities succeeds in solving the problem.
- At this level emphasis is laid on identifying the problem, defining it and finding a solution to it.
- The student's original thinking and creative-abilities develop at this level.
- The role of the teacher in this level of teaching is democratic. He does not force knowledge on the students but develops their talents and capabilities.
- The role of the students is quite active.
- Reflective level of teaching is that which is problem-centered and the student is busy in original imagination.
- The teaching at this level is not teacher-centered or subject-centered, it is leaner-centered.
- There is an interaction between the teacher and the taught at the reflective level teaching.
- At this level, teaching is appropriate for the higher class.
- At this level, teaching is highly thoughtful and useful than the teaching at the memory or understanding level.
- Not suitable for small children at the lower level of teaching. It is suitable only for mentally matured children.
- At this level, the study material is neither organized nor pre-planned. Therefore, students cannot acquire systematic and organized knowledge of their study courses.

4. Autonomous Development Level

Morris L. Biggie (1976) has added one more level under the rubric 'autonomous development'. It is the first level and is student-oriented and dependent on the learner's feelings and judgment i.e., Self-study.

Methods of teaching

Teacher Centred Methods	Learner-Centred Method
The main focus is on the teacher मुख्य फोकस शिक्षक पर है	On student छात्र पर
Passive Learners निष्क्रिय शिक्षार्थी	Active Learners सक्रिय शिक्षार्थी
Flexibility नम्यता	अधिक ग्रेटर लचीलापन More Greater Flexibility
Student work on own not groups विद्यार्थी स्वयं समूहों पर काम करते है	छात्र समूहों पर काम करते हैं Student work on groups
Teacher monitors students शिक्षक छात्रों की निगरानी करता है।	Student can Learn even विद्यार्थी भी सीख सकते हैं

Teacher Chooses the topic , study material, classroom, AND no have choice शिक्षक विषय, अध्ययन सामग्री, कक्षा का चयन करता है, और कोई विकल्प नहीं है	Student Have Choice study material, Learning active ,timeline, स्टूडेंट के पास च्वाइस स्टडी मटीरियल, लर्निंग एक्टिव, टाइमलाइन
One way flow of Knowledge , from teacher to students एक तरह से ज्ञान का प्रवाह, शिक्षक से लेकर छात्रों तक	they have more then way flow of Knowledge उनके पास ज्ञान का प्रवाह अधिक है
Way of method-Classs, PPT etc विधि-वर्ग, पीपीटी आदि का तरीका	Way of method Tutorial, Assignment ,Project etc विधि का तरीका ट्यूटोरियल, असाइनमेंट, प्रोजेक्ट आदि

Teacher-centered strategy	Mixed strategy	Learner-centered strategy
Large group method	Small group methods	Individualized
1. Lectures	1. Group discussion	1. Tutorials
2. Team teaching	2. Seminar	2. Assignments
3. TV or video presentation	3. Panel discussion	3. Project work
	4. Brainstorming	4. Case study
	5. Project method or work	5. Programmed instruction
	6. Tutorials	6. Computer-assigned learning
	7. Case study	7. Interactive video
	8. Role play	8. Open learning
	9. Simulation	9. Personalized system of instruction (PSI)
	10. Demonstration	10. Heuristic method

THE LECTURE METHOD

A formal or semi-formal discourse in which the instructor presents a series of events, facts, or principles, explores a problem, or explains relationships

- It creates new ideas.
- It is good for a large class.
- The teacher is experienced and has mastery of the subject, explains all points, and can answer all questions raised by students.

THE DISCUSSION METHOD

- A method in which group discussion techniques are used to reach instructional objectives
- Students listen to other's opinions & express their own.
- Students exchange their ideas.
- when students give their ideas, the teacher corrects their mistakes.
- Students can make their own notes

Programmed Instruction

Programmed Instruction (PI) is a general term for a highly structured system of learning, which is based on the logical sequence of self-paced, learning steps with feedback between each step. The learner gets immediate feedback after each step i.e., Automated book

THE STUDY ASSIGNMENT METHOD

- A method in which the instructor assigns reading to books, periodicals, project or research papers or exercises for the practice
- To orient students to a topic prior to classroom or Laboratory work.
- It enhances the ability to research any topic as the students search topic from different books.

THE TUTORIAL METHOD

- A method of instruction in which an instructor works directly with an individual student.
- To reach highly complicated skills operations or operations involving danger or expensive equipment.
- To provide individualized remedial assistance

THE DEMONSTRATION METHOD

- A method of instruction where the instructor by actually performing an operation or doing a job shows the students what to do, and how to do it, and through explanations brings out why, where, and when it is done.

Team teaching method:

- Team teaching is an innovative approach to teaching large groups in which two or more teachers are involved in planning, executing, and evaluating the learning experiences for a group of students

TV or Video Presentation

- Television or video presentation is an improved presentation of radio or audio presentation and it can virtually bring the whole world inside the classroom. Screening of video presentation is followed by a discussion or task.

Seminar:

- It is a type of group discussion where one trainee or several, prepare a paper on a given topic, issue, or problem, which is then presented to the whole group for discussion and analysis.

Panel-Discussion:

- A panel consists of a small group of six to eight people. For example, a panel discussion takes place on the issue of climate change. The leader must, in addition, take special care to select panel members who can think and speak effectively.

Brainstorming

- Brainstorming is a creative group work in which the group members produce a large number of ideas quickly on a given topic or problem for subsequent evaluation. In this method, anyone can exchange remarks with anyone except that the participants are not allowed to criticize the ideas at the time when views are being invented. Sometimes the quantity of ideas is more important than the quality. Spontaneously is the hallmark of brainstorming sessions.
- Unlike, a buzz session, brainstorming can work well in a large group and usually takes less time. Under buzz groups, judgment is given on ideas. So it is time-consuming.

Project Method:

- This can be described as both a small group and an individualized instruction. In this method, the students are allowed to explore and experience their environment through their senses and direct their own learning by their individual interests. Very little is taught from the textbooks and the emphasis is on experimental learning rather than rote learning and memorization.

Role-playing:

- Role playing has been used effectively by teachers to help solve classroom interpersonal problems and to teach human-relations skills in the classroom. Role-playing also been used to facilitate subject-matter learning through the dramatization of literary and historical works and historical and current events.

Stimulation

- Stimulation means creating conditions that are quite similar to actual conditions and then training is provided under those conditions. For example, the training of pilots and astronauts takes place in conditions that are quite similar to actual flight conditions. Stimulation is specifically used for training purposes.

Computer-assisted Learning

- Computer-assisted Learning (CAL) is concerned with the use of computers to mediate the flow of information in a learning process. A computer has the ability to process information very quickly, and accurately and to adapt and respond to the learner's needs, difficulties, and progress, which is much greater than that of a book or videotape.

Playway method

- Froebel believed that play is the principal means of learning in early childhood. In the play, children construct their understanding of the world through direct experience with it. The Froebel Trust champions children's play. Play helps children to see how they connect with nature and the world around them.

Heuristic Method

- This method was advocated by Professor Armstrong. In this method, the student has to find out the answer to his/her own problem with unaided efforts. Thus, the child becomes a discoverer of knowledge by developing a spirit of inquiry. The main aim of teaching by this method is not to provide many facts about Science, Mathematics, Grammar, etc., but to teach how knowledge of these can be obtained i.e., trial and error method.

Key behaviors of teaching

- Borich states that there is five key behaviour that makes effective teachers:
- **Lesson clarity**: idea should be clear to all learners at all levels. Ideas should be conveyed in a clear step-by-step order, they should be uncomplicated and with minimal distraction.
- **Instructional variety**: use a variety of teaching tools (technology, materials, activities, space, and displays). Use a variation in voice and gestures, rewards, and reinforcement.
- **Teacher task orientation**: to maximize the time spent teaching, be sure to handle inevitable interruptions quickly, expedite the giving and collecting of materials, prevent or quickly put an end to distracting behaviour, organize lessons well, and establish smooth transition.
- **Engagement in the learning process**: constantly monitor any seat work and group work, set rules for when students can leave class without disruption, keep a daily schedule to minimize confusion among students, and give independent work that is interesting.
- **Student success rate:** students should spend about 60-70% of their time on tasks that allow an almost complete understanding of the material being taught with only occasional errors. The content should reflect prior learning, with easy-to-grasp steps for the new material.

According to Borich, there is five **helpful behaviour** for effective teaching. They are:

- **Using student ideas and contribution**: teachers should use mediated dialogues and be sure to acknowledge, modify, apply, compare, and summarize student responses as necessary.
- **Structuring**: Teachers should reinforce the learned content and place it in relation to new content. Teachers should give organized lessons of what is to come and summarize what has been taught. (Advance organizers and summaries).
- **Questioning**: Use a variety of questions, and be sure to include questions that require more thinking and problem-solving.
- **Probing**: Draw more out of student responses by getting students to elaborate on their ideas (elicit clarification, solicit additional information, and redirecting the discussion). Help the student to discover the content rather than being explicitly told.
- **Teacher affects**: Develop the teacher- learner relationship by the use of enthusiasm (inflection in voice and movement, gesturing, and eye contact.

Factors affecting teaching

Related to teacher

- **A teacher should have the following qualities.**
- Personal qualities like warmth affectionate, Sympathetic, Democratic optimistic, etc.
- Professional competencies like command on the subject matter, effective communication, proper use of teaching, instruction facilities, and classroom.

From the training point of view, we can classify teaching skills into three broad Categories.

- Core teaching skills (Common for all subjects)
- Specific teaching skills (For specific subject areas like language, social science, science, math, etc.)
- Target group-specific skills (For exceptional children)

Learner related factors

- **Learner's attitude such as**
- More intensity of learning
- Joyful learning
- Self-directed learning
- Self-motivated learning
- Background knowledge of the learner
- Nature of learning material
- Motivation
- Learning support
- Qualities and traits of learners such as. Level of intelligence, attitude, motivation, learning style, aptitude, readiness to take risks, etc. can impact the way they learn.

Related to Supporting material.

- Support material is very essential, which affects the teaching-learning process.
- It is an important resource in teaching, support material includes textbooks, magazines, journals, periodicals, practice questions, teacher solution manuals, etc.
- The support materials aim to support teachers and students in achieving the learning outcome of any subject.

Related to Instructional facilities.

- Instructional facilities that assist an instructor in the teaching-learning process.
- Instructional facilities play a great role in the effective teaching-learning process.
- The teaching institutional facilities include Karma TV, radio, tape recorder, projectors, film strips, Internet, and so on.

Related to Institutional and administrative setup.

- Administrative setup with variety and freedom of choice for the teacher generates a healthy teaching environment. Teachers are free to prepare their lesson plans and use a variety of teaching aids.

- In the teaching process administrative discipline of the institution should be followed while the administrative pressure should be avoided.
- Administrative setup of the institution should be designed in such a manner so that a balance of the relationship between teacher-student, teacher-parent, among teachers, and school staff should be ensured.

Learner's characteristics;

- **Personal characteristics** often relate to demographic information such as age gender, maturation language, social economic status, cultural background, and specific needs of a learner group such as particular skills and disabilities for and/or impairments to learning.
- **Academic characteristics** are more education and learning related such as learning goals (of an Individual or a group), prior knowledge, educational type, and educational level.
- **Social/emotional characteristics** relate to the group or to the individual respect to the group, Examples of social/emotional characteristics are group structure, place of the individual within a group, sociability, self-image (also feelings of self-efficacy and agency), mood, etc.
- **Cognitive characteristics** relate to such things as attention span, memory, mental procedures, and intellectual skills which determine how the learner perceives, remembers, thinks, solves problems, organizes, and represents information in her/his brain.
- Readiness to learn/Desire to learn, Motivation, interest & curiosity to learn.
- Attitudes & Habits: Must be positive & encouraging.
- Academic skills: Acquiring academic skills is the most important quality of a good student.
- Absence of anger & Jealousy: They have weaker learning abilities
- Perceptiveness: A good student always perceives the right meaning from conversations
- Self-Discipline
- Understanding
- Slow beginning followed by the gradual development of interests.

Adolescence, a transitional phase of growth and development between childhood and adulthood, The World Health Organization (WHO) defines an adolescent as any person between ages 10 and 19 This age range falls within WHO's definition of young people which refers to individuals between ages 10 and 24.

- "An adult is a person older than 19 years of age unless national law defines a person as being an adult at an earlier age." By WHO
- "An infant is a child younger than one year of age. "WHO"

Characteristics of adolescent

- **Intellectual development includes**
- Moving from concrete to abstract thinking.
- High achievement when challenged and engaged.
- An intense curiosity and wide range of intellectual pursuit, few of which are sustained over the long term.

- An ability to be self-reflective. Prefers active over passive learning experiences
- Demand the relevance in foaming and what is being taught.
- Interest in interacting with peers during learning activities.

Physical development includes:

- Restlessness and fatigue due to hormonal changes.
- A need for physical activity because of increased energy.
- A concern with changes in body size and shape.
- Physical vulnerability resulting from poor health/dietary habits or engaging in risky behaviors.
- Bodily changes that may cause awkward, uncoordinated movements.

Emotional and psychological development includes:

- A Mood swings marked by peaks of intensity and by unpredictability.
- Needing to release energy, with sudden outbursts of activity.
- A desire to become independent and to search for adult identity and acceptance.
- Self-consciousness and being sensitive to personal criticism.
- A Concern about physical growth and maturity.
- A belief that their personal problems, feelings, and experiences are unique to themselves.
- Overreacting to ridicule, embarrassment, and rejection.
- Seeking approval of peers and others with attention-getting behaviors.

Social development includes:

- Modelling behavior after that of older students, not necessarily that of parents and other adults.
- Seeking approval of peers and others with attention-getting behaviors.
- Overreacting to ridicule, embarrassment, and rejection.

Moral development includes:

- An understanding of the complexity of moral issues (question values, cultural expressions, and religious teachings).
- Being capable of and interested in participating in democracy.
- Impatience with the pace of change, and underestimating how difficult it is to make social changes.
- Needing and being influenced by **adult role models** who will listen and be trustworthy.
- Relying on parents and important adults for advice, but wanting to make their own decisions.
- Judging others quickly, but acknowledging one's own faults slowly.

Characteristics of adult learners;

- **Autonomy -** Adults typically prefer a sense of control and self-direction. They like options and choices in their learning environment.
- **Goal-oriented -** Many adults have specific goals they are trying to achieve. They prefer to partake in learning activities that help them reach their goals.
- Wealth of Knowledge in the journey from childhood to adulthood, people accumulate a

unique store of knowledge and experiences. They bring this depth and breadth of knowledge to the learning situation.

- **Purposeful -** Workplace training is often part of an initiative that involves change. Adults want to know the purpose of training and the motivation underlying an organization's training initiative.
- **Emotional Barriers -** Through experience, adults may fear a subject, have anxiety about a subject or feel anger about forced changes in job responsibilities or policies. These emotions can interfere with the learning process.
- **Practical -** Adults in the workplace prefer practical knowledge and experiences that will make work easier or provide important skills.
- **Competence and mastery -** Adults like to gain competence in workplace skills as it boosts confidence and improves self-esteem.
- **Learning by experience -** Many adults prefer to learn by doing rather than listening to lectures.
- **Results-oriented -** Adults are results-oriented. They have specific expectations for what they will get out of learning activities and will often drop out of voluntary learning if their expectations aren't met.
- **Big Picture -** Adults require the big picture view of what they're learning. They need to know how the small parts fit into the larger landscape.
- **Responsible for Self** - Adult learners often take responsibility for their own success or failure at learning.
- **Need for Community -** Many self-directed adult learners prefer a learning community with whom they can interact and discuss questions and issues.
- **Outside responsibilities -** Most adult learners have numerous responsibilities and commitments to family, friends, community, and work. Carving out time for learning affects adult learners.
- **Potential physical limitations -** Depending on their age and physical condition, adult learners may acquire psychomotor skills more slowly than younger students and have more difficulties reading small fonts and seeing small images on the computer screen.

Field Independent Learners	Field Dependent Learners
• Analytic, competitive, independent, and individualistic • Self-defined goals, strategies, and reinforcement • Intrinsically motivated • Poor social skills/prefer individual projects • Well organized and structured in their learning • Autonomous in cognitive restructuring skills	• Sensitive to environments • Easily influenced by prevailing field or context • Group oriented, global, and socially-sensitive/prefer group project • Prefer externally defined goals and reinforcements, and clear definitions of desired outcomes • Extrinsically motivated • Less structured, less autonomous

Bloom's Domains of Learning

- In 1956, American educational psychologist, Benjamin Bloom, first proposed three domains of learning; cognitive, affective and psycho-motor. Bloom worked in collaboration with David Krathwohl and Anne Harrow throughout the 1950s-70s on the three domains.

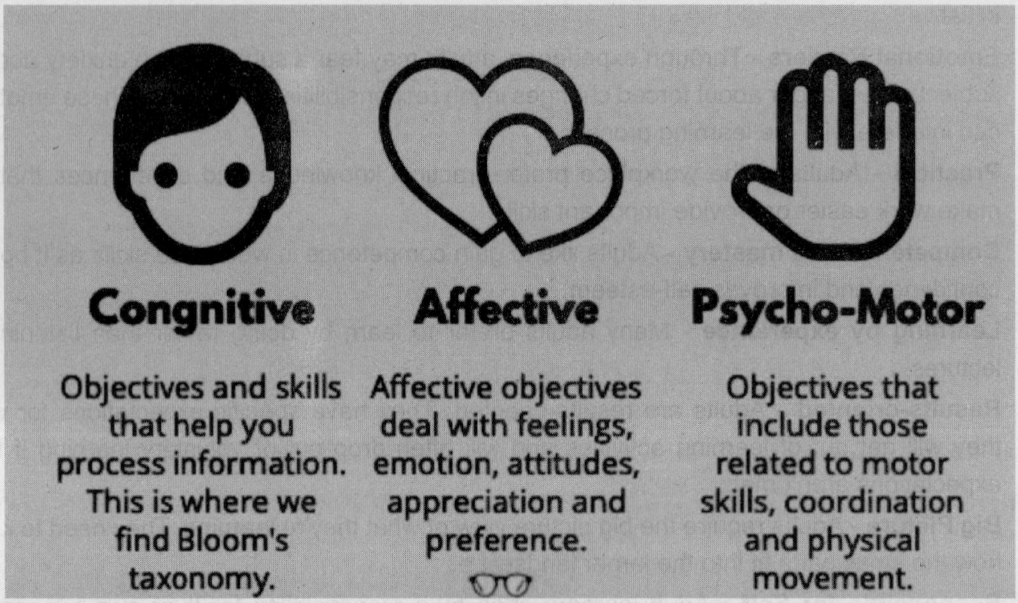

The Cognitive Domain (Bloom's Taxonomy)

- This was the first domain to be proposed in 1956 and it focuses on the idea that objectives that are related to cognition could be divided into subdivisions and ranked in order of cognitive difficulty.
- These ranked subdivisions are what we commonly refer to as Bloom's taxonomy.
- However, there was a major revision of the subdivisions in 2000-01 by Bloom's original partner, David Krathwohl and his colleague, Lorin Anderson (Anderson was a former student of Bloom's).
- The highlights of this revision were switching names of the subdivisions from nouns to verbs, thus making them easier to use when curriculum and lesson planning.
- The other main change was the order of the top two subdivisions was reversed.

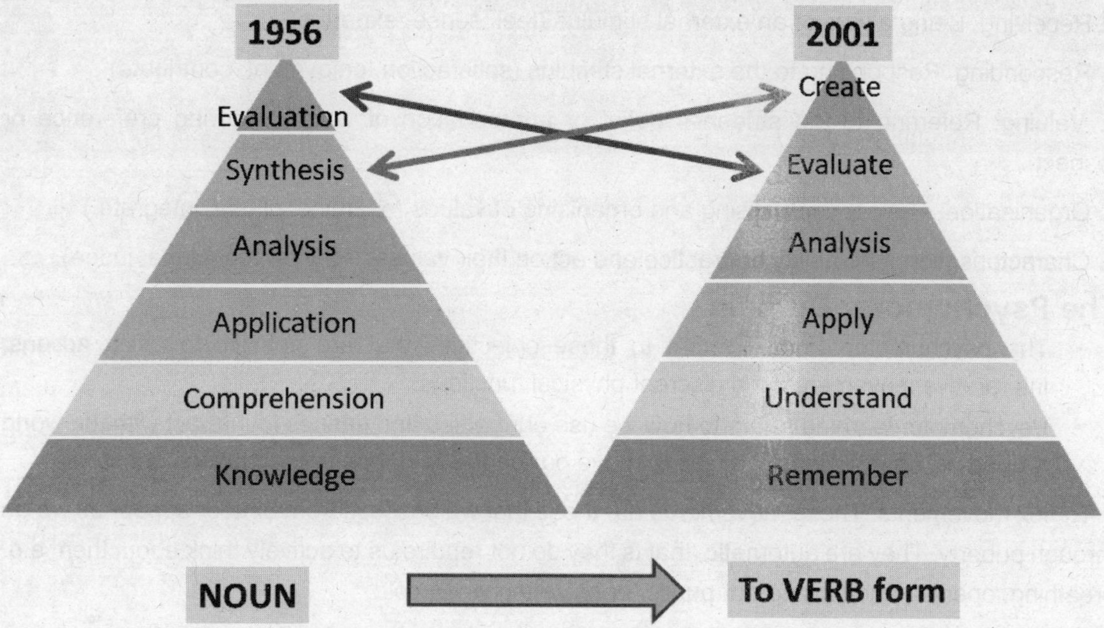

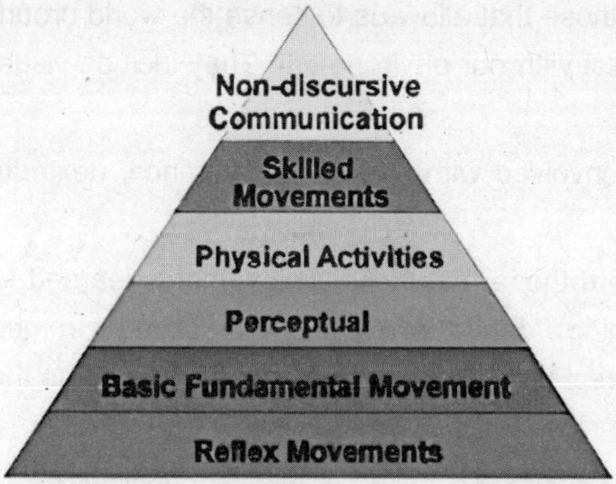

Psychomotor

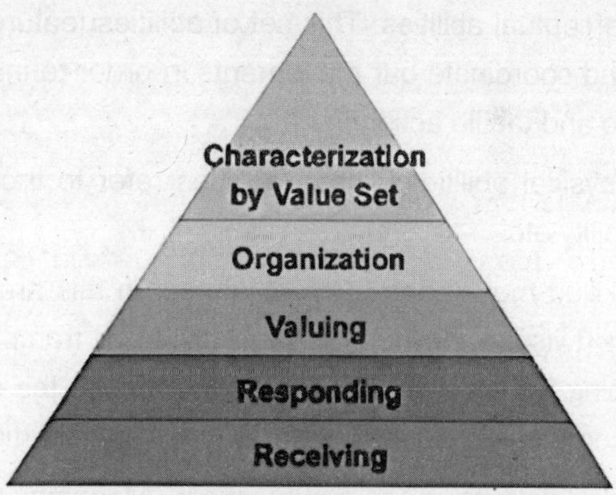

Affective

The Affective Domain

- The affective domain (sometimes referred to as the feeling domain) is concerned with feelings and emotions and also divides objectives into hierarchical subcategories. It was proposed by Krathwohl and Bloom in 1964.
- The affective domain is not usually used when planning for maths and sciences as feelings and emotions are not relevant for those subjects. However, for educators of arts and

language, the inclusion of the affective domain is imperative wherever possible.

The ranked domain subcategories range from "receiving" at the lower end up to "characterisation" at the top. The full ranked list is as follows:

1. Receiving. Being aware of an external stimulus (feel, sense, experience).

2. Responding. Responding to the external stimulus (satisfaction, enjoyment, contribute)

3. Valuing. Referring to the student's belief or appropriation of worth (showing preference or respect).

4. Organisation. The conceptualising and organising of values (examine, clarify, integrate.)

5. Characterisation. The ability to practice and act on their values. (Review, conclude, judge).

The Psychomotor Domain

- The psychomotor domain refers to those objectives that are specific to reflex actions, interpretive movements and discreet physical functions.
- Psychomotor learning refers to how we use our bodies and senses to interact with the world around us, such as learning how to move our bodies in dance or gymnastics.

1. Reflex movements. These movements are those that we possess from birth or appear as we go through puberty. They are automatic, that is they do not require us to actively think about them e.g. breathing, opening and closing our pupils, or shivering when cold.

2. Fundamental movements. These are those actions that are the basic movements, running, jumping, walking, etc, and commonly form part of more complex actions such as playing a sport.

3. Perceptual abilities. This set of abilities features those that allow us to sense the world around us and coordinate our movements in order to interact with our environment. They include visual, audio and tactile actions.

4. Physical abilities. These abilities refer to those involved with strength, endurance, dexterity, flexibility etc.

5. Skilled movements. Objectives set in this area are those that include movements learned for sport (twisting the body in high diving or trampolining), dance, or playing a musical instrument (placing fingers on guitar strings to produce the correct note). It is through these movements that we sometimes use the layman's term "muscle memory".

6. Non-discursive communication. Meaning communication without writing, non-discursive communication refers to physical actions such as facial expressions, posture, and gestures.

Skinner's Behaviorist Theory

Operant Conditioning

Operant conditioning is based on Thorndike's "Law of Effect" (1898), in which it is proposed that behaviors that are followed by positive responses are likely to be repeated and those that are followed by negative responses, not repeated.

Skinner refined the Law of Effect by introducing "reinforcement" into the descriptions. Using Skinner's new description we end up with; those behaviors that are reinforced are repeated (strengthened) and those not reinforced tend to dissipate (are weakened).

Positive Reinforcement

- From a class`room management perspective, positive reinforcement is an essential strategy for teaching students how to act and conduct themselves. Positive reinforcement (e.g. praise) should be given for behaviors that are desirable, for example, verbally answering questions in class. Initially, this should be done for all answers given, regardless of whether they are correct. This will build a culture of answering questions.
- As the behavior in question becomes commonplace, the teacher should then both reduce the frequency of the reinforcement and, as in our above example, only give it for correct answers.
- Ultimately the teacher will reduce the frequency of the positive reinforcement to only those responses of the highest calibre. This will create a culture of desired excellence in the students.

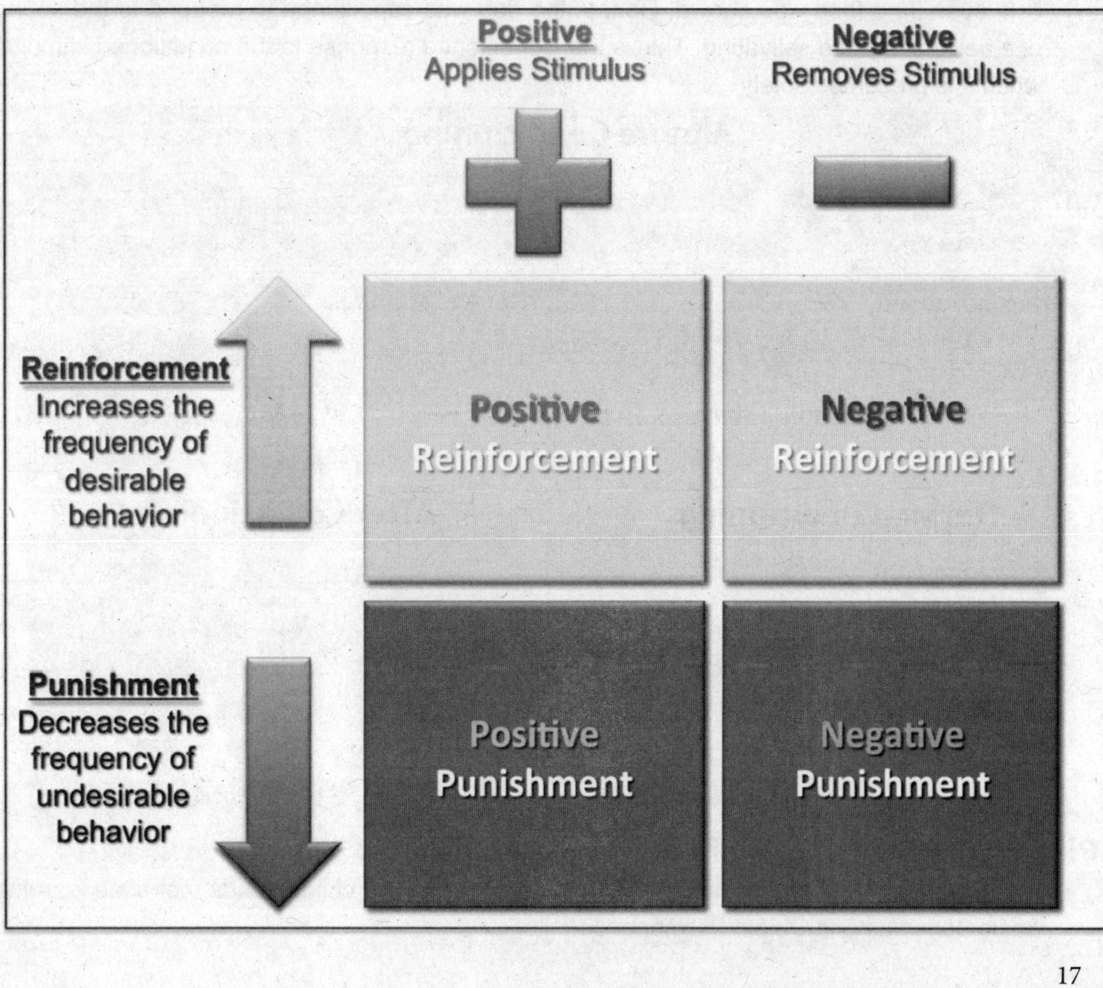

Classical conditioning theory

- Classical conditioning is the relationship of one event with another and desired event resulting in behaviour.
- Developed on the basis of experiments by Ivan Pavlov, the Russian psychologist who tried to establish a Stimulus-Response (S-R) connection/link.
- In his experiment, he correlated the dog's salivation and the ringing of the bell. Pavlov carried out his experiment in three stages.
- Stage I: The dog is provided with a piece of meat, the dog shows a noticeable increment in salivation. Here, the meat is an unconditional stimulus which is biologically effective and salivation is an unconditional response to the unconditioned stimulus which is an unlearned response.
- Stage II: In this stage, rather than giving a piece of meat the dog was unveiled with the sound of the ringing bell; the dog did not salivate to the mere sound of a ringing bell.
- Stage III: In order to build the relationship, he repeated the presentation of meat and the ringing of a bell frequently. After some time, the dog began to salivate whenever the bell rang. After repeating the same process, the dog started salivating just at the sound of the bell, even if no food was shown. Hence, the dog was conditioned to respond to the sound of a bell and started salivating. This is the Conditioned response to the conditioned stimulus when it is presented solely

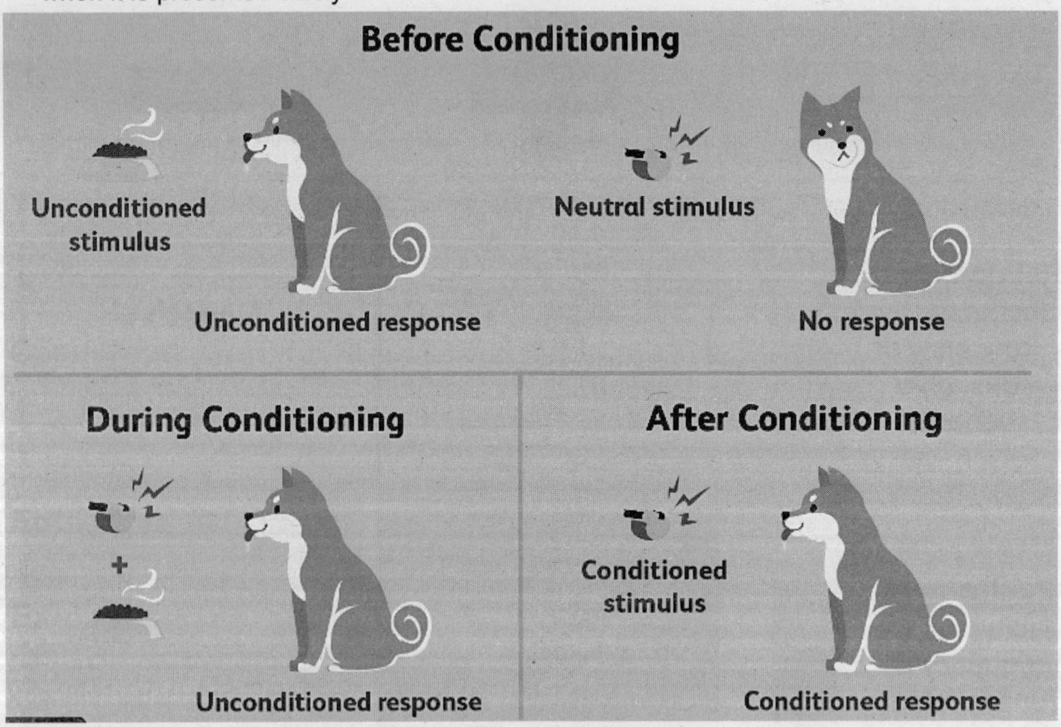

Piaget's Theory of Cognitive Development

- The Sensorimotor Stage runs from birth to 2 years and the child spends their time learning basic Schemas and Object Permanence

- The Preoperational Stage runs from 2 years to 7 years and the child develops more Schemas and the ability to think Symbolically.
- The Concrete Operational Stage runs from 7 years to 11 years and this is the Stage when children start to work things out in their head rather than physically in the real world.
- The Formal Operational Stage runs from 11 years into adulthood and this is where abstract thought develops, as does logic and cool stuff like hypothesis testing.
- According to Piaget, the whole process is active and requires the rediscovery and reconstructing of knowledge across the entire process of Stages.

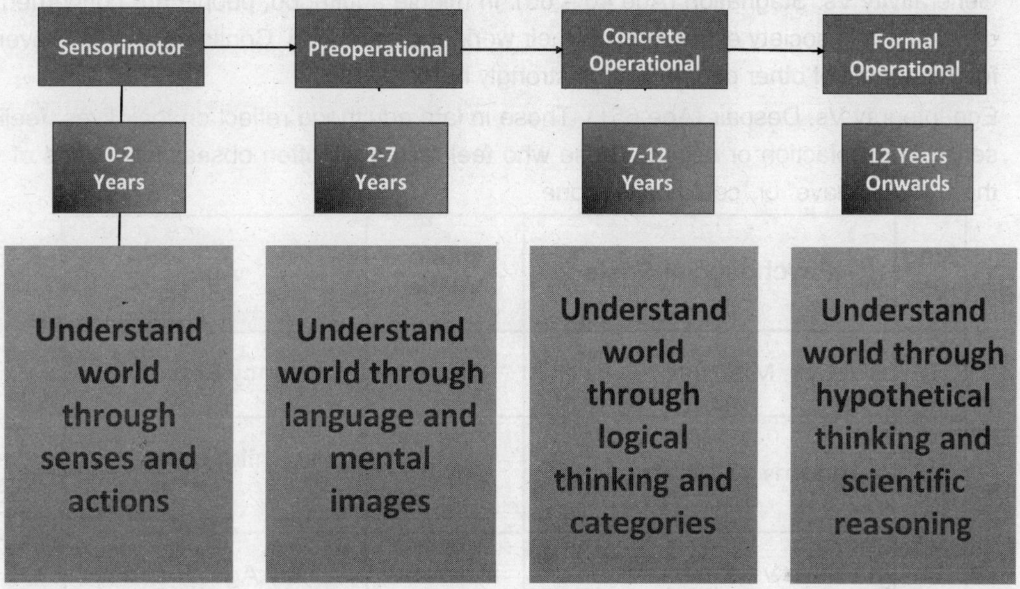

Erikson's 8 Stages of Psychological Development

- According to Erikson, we experience eight stages of development during our life span. Within each stage, there is a dilemma that we must resolve in order to feel a sense of competence and will allow us to develop as a well-adjusted adult.

Erikson's 8 Stages

- Trust Vs. Mistrust (Age 0 – 1.5). In this first stage, infants must learn that adults can be trusted. If treated poorly children may grow up feeling mistrust towards people.
- Autonomy Vs. Shame (Age 1.5 – 3). The "me do it' stage, children start to make decisions and show preferences of elements in their environment such as what clothes to wear or what toy they prefer. If children are not allowed to explore these preferences they may develop low self-esteem and shame.
- Initiative Vs. Guilt (Age 3 – 5). This stage involves children learning to plan and achieve goals involving others. If parents or teachers allow children to explore this and support their choices they will develop a sense of purpose and strong self-confidence.
- Industry Vs. Inferiority (Age 5 – 12). In this stage, children start comparing themselves with

their peers. Success at this will result in a sense of accomplishment in their school work, social and family activities and sports.

- Identity Vs. Role Confusion (Age 12 – 18). Students in this stage are asking themselves "Who am I" and "What do I want to do in my life". They will try out multiple roles during this time to find what one "fits" best. A strong sense of identity and an ability to defend their core beliefs in the face of other opinions would be considered success at this stage.
- Intimacy Vs. Isolation (Age 18 – 40). As students progress into early adulthood their focus shifts to making and maintaining strong, intimate relationships with others.
- Generativity Vs. Stagnation (Age 40 – 65). In middle adulthood, people are concerned with contributing to society either through their work or parenthood. Continued self-improvement for the benefit of other people figures strongly here.
- Ego Integrity Vs. Despair (Age 65+). Those in late adulthood reflect on their lives, feeling a sense of satisfaction or failure. Those who feel failure wil often obsess with ideas of what they "should have" or "could have" done.

Stage	**Psychosocial Crisis**	**Basic Virtue**	**Age**
1.	Trust vs. Mistrust	Hope	Infancy (0 to 1½)
2.	Autonomy vs. Shame	Will	Early Childhood (1½ to 3)
3.	Initiative vs. Guilt	Purpose	Play Age (3 to 5)
4.	**Industry vs. Inferiority**	**Competency**	**School Age (5 to 12)**
5.	Ego identity vs. Role Confusion	Fidelity	Adolescence (12 to 18)
6.	Intimacy vs. Isolation	Love	Young Adult (18 to 40)
7.	Generative vs. Stagnation	Care	Adulthood (40 to 65)
8.	Ego integrity vs. Despair	Wisdom	Maturity (65)

Maslow's Need Hierarchy Theory

- Maslow's Need Hierarchy Theory is one of the Motivation Theory.
- Abraham Harold Maslow advocated the theory of motivation based on various needs.

- Maslow identified five distinct categories of needs.
- He arranged these needs into a hierarchy.
- Stated that individuals wish to satisfy a particular need to a moderate extent, and then try to satisfy the next need in the hierarchy.
- Maslow identified human needs into five distinct categories:
  1. Physiological Needs
  2. Safety Needs
  3. Social Needs
  4. Esteem Needs
  5. Self-actualization Needs

Given below is Maslows' Hierarchy of needs.

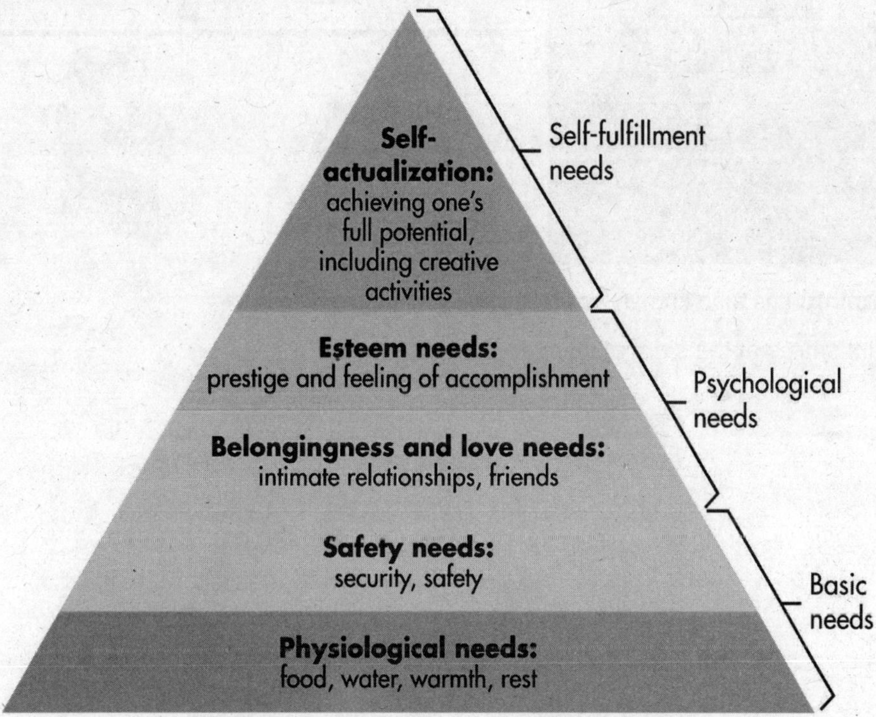

Gagne Hierarchy of learning

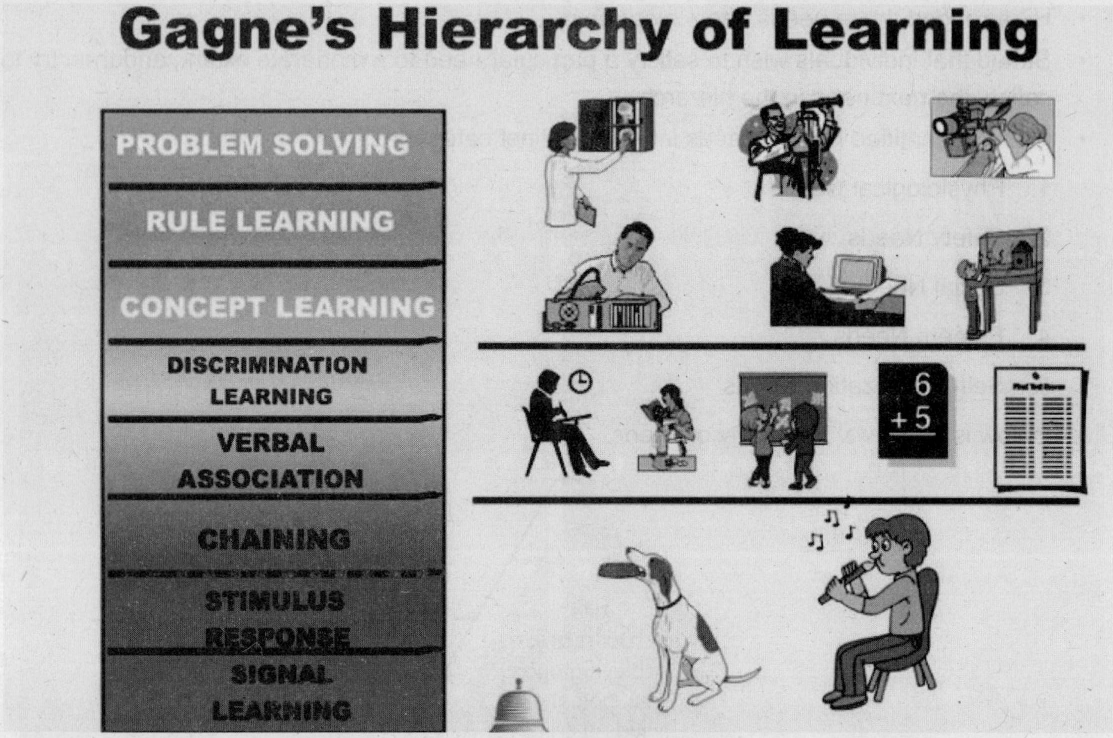

Signal learning: It is also known as classical conditioning.

Ex: An infant smiles at the sight of its mother.

Stimulus-Response Learning (Operant Conditioning)

- Involves the connection between a stimulus and a response. The learner is learning to make precise movements of muscle in response to specific stimuli.
- Eg. A child says papa at the sight of his father

Chain Learning

- This is a more advanced form of learning in which the subject develops the ability to connect two or more previously learned stimulus response bonds into a linked sequence.

- It is the process whereby most complex psychomotor skills (eg: riding a bicycle or playing the piano) are learned.

Verbal associate learning: Mediating connections between each verbal unit and the next must have been previously learned.

- Example: A child learns the Malayalam equivalent of English words.

Multiple discrimination: Discrimination involves higher mental processes

- Example: The child learns to distinguish between his mother and his aunt.

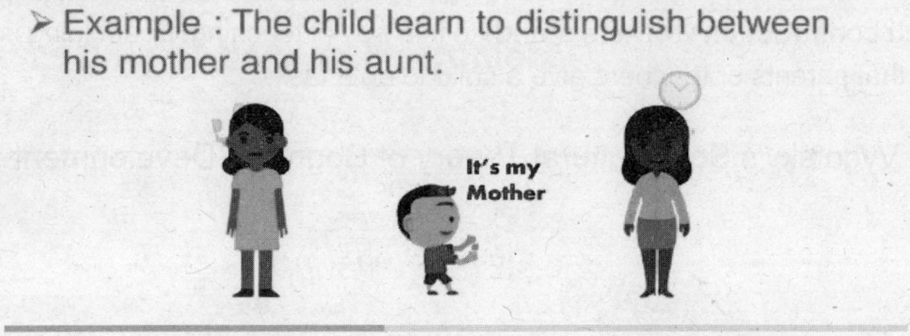

Concept learning: A concept is a class of stimuli, which have common characteristics. We form concepts by finding properties that a class of objects shares in common. Example: The child learns the concept bird. He distinguishes a bird from a mammal.

Learning of principle: Learning of principle depends upon learning of concept formation and another form of learning. Principles show the regular relationship between two or more concepts.

- Example: A child learns the principle – metals expand on heating.

Problem-solving: This comes at the highest stage in the hierarchy of the learning process. It depends on learning rules. It constitutes the use of the 'discovery method'.

- Example: A boy proves theorems in geometry.

Vygotsky theory of learning

- **Vygotsky (1896-1934)** was a Russian psychologist who argued that culture has a major impact on a child's cognitive development.
- He believed that social interactions with adults and more learned peers can facilitate a child's potential for learning. Without this interpersonal instruction, he believed children's minds

would not advance very far as their knowledge would be based only on their own discoveries.

- **Zone of Proximal Development and Scaffolding**: Vygotsky's best-known concept is the Zone of Proximal Development (ZPD). Vygotsky stated that children should be taught in the ZPD, which occurs when they can almost perform a task, but not quite on their own without assistance. With the right kind of teaching, however, they can accomplish it successfully. A good teacher identifies a child's ZPD and helps the child stretch beyond it.
- Then the adult (teacher) gradually withdraws support until the child can then perform the task unaided. Researchers have applied the metaphor of **scaffolds (the temporary platforms on which construction workers stand)** to this way of teaching. Scaffolding is the temporary support that parents or teachers give a child to do a task.

Vygotsky's Sociocultural Theory of Cognitive Development

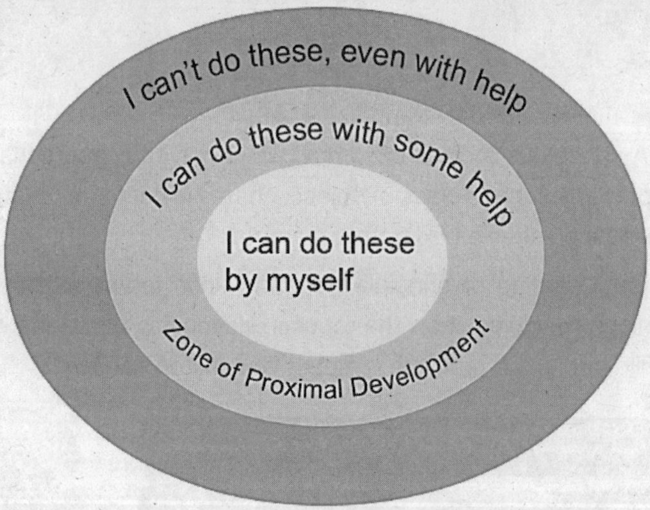

- **Contrast with Piaget:** Piaget was highly critical of teacher-directed instruction believing that teachers who take control of the child's learning place the child into a passive role (Crain, 2005). Further, teachers may present abstract ideas without the child's true understanding, and instead, they just repeat back what they heard. Piaget believed children must be given opportunities to discover concepts on their own. As previously stated, Vygotsky did not believe children could reach a higher cognitive level without instruction from more learned individuals.

Digital Initiatives in learning

MOOC'S

The concept of Massive Open Online Courses (MOOCs) involves online delivery of interactive learning content to large number of people simultaneously.

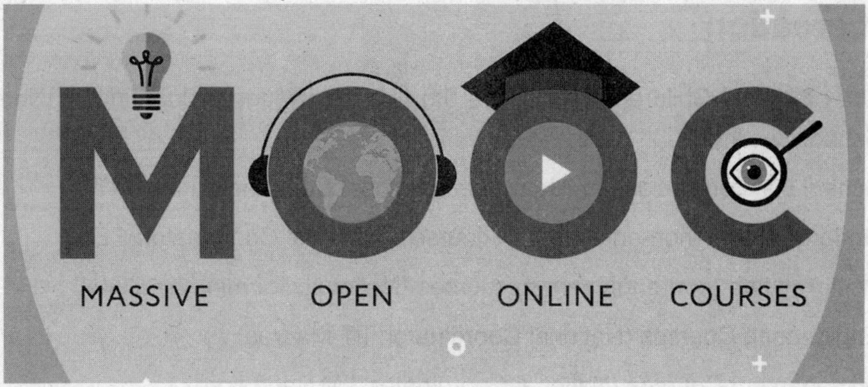

1. Study Webs of Active Learning for Young Aspiring Mind (SWAYAM)

SWAYAM is an indigenous (Made in India) IT Massive Open Online Courses (MOOCs) Platform for providing best quality education that can be accessed by anyone, anytime and anywhere using the IT system.

- Study Webs of Active Learning for Young Aspiring Minds (SWAYAM), was launched on July 9, 2017 by the Ministry of Human Resource Development to provide one integrated platform and portal for online courses.
- This covers all higher education subjects and skill sector courses.
- The objective is to ensure that every student in the country has access to the best quality higher education at the affordable cost.
- designed to achieve the three cardinal principles of Education Policy viz., access, equity and quality.
- SWAYAM seeks to bridge the digital divide for students who have hitherto remained untouched by the digital revolution and have not been able to join the mainstream of the knowledge economy.
- Academicians from hundreds of institutions throughout the country are involved in developing & delivering Massive open online courses (MOOCs) through SWAYAM in almost all disciplines from senior schooling to Post Graduation.
  a) Video tutorials covering a whole course
  b) E-Content reading material that could add to the learning imparted through the tutorials.
  c) Self-Assessment: Quizzes/assignments that intersperse the course
  d) Discussion forum for posting queries.

2. SWAYAM Prabha:

The SWAYAM PRABHA is a group of 34 DTH channels devoted to telecasting of high-quality educational programmes on 24X7 basis using the GSAT-15 satellite. Every day, there will be new content for at least (4) hours which would be repeated 5 more times in a day, allowing the students to choose the time of their convenience. The channels are uplinked from BISAG, Gandhinagar. The contents are provided by NPTEL, IITs, UGC, CEC, IGNOU. The INFLIBNET Centre maintains the web portal.

Content creation

(a). Out of school Children: for classes 9th to 12th (National Coordinator: National Open School Society).

(b). School children in classes 9th to 12th (National Coordinator: NCERT)

(c). Undergraduate (non-engineering) courses (National Coordinator: CEC)

(d). Postgraduate (non-engineering) courses (National Coordinator: UGC).

(e). Engineering Courses (National Coordinator: IIT Madras)

(f). Management Courses (National Coordinator: IIM Bangalore)

(g). Out-of-college students (National Coordinator: IGNOU).

(h). Teaching the teachers (National Coordinator: NITTER Chennai).

Choice Based Credit System (CBCS)

- Choice-Based Credit System: The CBCS provides an opportunity for the students to choose courses from the prescribed courses comprising core, elective/minor or skill-based courses. The courses can be evaluated following the grading system, which is considered to be better than the conventional marks system.
- Therefore, it is necessary to introduce a uniform grading system in the entire higher education in India. This will benefit the students to move across institutions within India, to begin with, and across countries.

Advantages of the Choice-Based Credit System

The advantage of Choice Based Credit System (CBCS) are the followings:

- Shift in focus from teacher-centric to student- centric education.
- Student may undertake as many credits as they can cope with (without repeating all courses in a given semester if they fail in one/more courses).
- CBCS allows students to choose inter-disciplinary, intra-disciplinary courses, skill-oriented papers (even from other disciplines according to their learning needs, interests and aptitude) and more flexibility for students).
- CBCS makes education broad-based and at par with global standards. One can take credits by combining unique combinations. For example, Physics with Economics, Microbiology with Chemistry or Environment Science etc.
- CBCS offers flexibility for students to study at different times and at different institutions to complete one course (ease mobility of students). Credits earned at one institution can be transferred.

Disadvantages:

- Difficult to estimate the exact marks
- Workload of teachers may fluctuate
- Demand good infrastructure for dissemination of education

Applicability of the Grading System

- These guidelines shall apply to all undergraduate and postgraduate level degree, diploma and certificate programmes under the credit system awarded by the Central, State and Deemed to be universities in India.

Types of Courses

Courses in a programme may be of three kinds: Core, Elective and Foundation.

1. Core Course: There may be a Core Course in every semester. This is the course that is to be compulsorily studied by a student as a core requirement to complete the requirement of a programme in a said discipline of study.

2. **Elective Course**: Elective course is a course which can be chosen from a pool of papers.

It may be:

- Supportive to the discipline of study
- Providing an expanded scope
- Enabling an exposure to some other discipline/domain
- Nurturing student's proficiency/skill.

Letter Grades and Grade Points

A. **Two methods** -relative grading or absolute grading- have been in vogue for awarding grades in a course. The relative grading is based on the distribution (usually normal distribution) of marks obtained by all the students of the course and the grades are awarded based on a cut- off marks or percentile. Under the absolute grading, the marks are converted to grades based on pre-determined class intervals. To implement the following grading system, the colleges and universities can use any one of the above methods.

B. The UGC recommends a 10-point grading system with the following letter grades as given below:

Grades and Grade Points

Letter Grade	Grade Point
O (Outstanding)	10
A+(Excellent)	9
A (Very Good)	8
B+(Good)	7
B(Above Average)	6
C(Average)	5
P (Pass)	4
F(Fail)	0
Ab (Absent)	0

C. A student obtaining Grade F shall be considered failed and will be required to reappear in the examination.

C. A student obtaining a Grade F shall be considered failed and will be required to reappear in the examination.

D. For non-credit courses 'Satisfactory' or "Unsatisfactory' shall be indicated instead of the letter grade and this will not be counted for the computation of SGPA/CGPA.

E. The Universities can decide on the grade or percentage of marks required to pass in a course and also the CGPA required to qualify for a degree taking into consideration the recommendations of the statutory professional councils such as AICTE, MCI, BCI, NCTE etc.,

F. The statutory requirement for eligibility to enter as an assistant professor in colleges and universities in the disciplines of arts, science, commerce, etc., is a minimum average mark of 50% and 55% in relevant postgraduate degrees respectively for reserved and general categories.

Hence, it is recommended that the cut-off marks for grade B shall not be less than 50% and for grade B+, it should not be less than 55% under the absolute grading system. Similarly, cut-off marks shall be fixed for grades B and B+ based on the recommendation of the statutory bodies (AICTE, NCTE etc.,) of the relevant disciplines.

Key Words under CBCS:

- **Academic Year:** Two consecutive (one odd + one even) semesters constitute one academic year.
- **Choice-Based Credit System (CBCS):** The CBCS provides choices for students to select from the prescribed courses (core, elective or minor, or soft skill courses).
- **Course:** Usually referred to, as 'papers' is a component of a programme. All courses need not carry the same weight. The courses should define learning objectives and learning outcomes. A course may be designed to comprise lectures/tutorials/laboratory work/ field work/ outreach activities/project work/vocational training/viva/ seminars/ term papers/ assignments/ presentations/ self-study etc. or a combination of some of these.
- **Credit-Based Semester System (CBSS):** Under the CBSS, the requirement for awarding a degree or diploma, or certificate is prescribed in terms of the number of credits to be completed by the students
- **Credit Point:** It is the product of grade points and the number of credits for a course.
- **Credit:** A unit by which the coursework is measured. It determines the number of hours of instructions required per week. One credit is equivalent to one hour of teaching (lecture or tutorial) or two hours of practical work/field work per week.
- **Cumulative Grade Point Average (CGPA):** It is a measure of the overall cumulative performance of an index of a student over all semesters. The CGPA is the ratio of total credit points secured by a student in various courses in all semesters and the sum of the total credits of all courses in all semesters. It is expressed up to two decimal places.
- **Grade Point**: It is a numerical weight allotted to each letter grade on a 10-point scale.
- **Letter Grade**: It is x of the performance of students in a said course. Grades are denoted by letters O, A+, A, B+, B, C, P, and F.
- **Semester:** Each semester will consist of 15-18 weeks of academic work equivalent to 90

actual teaching days. The odd semester may be scheduled from July to December and even semester from January to June.

- **Transcript or Grade Card or Certificate:** Based on the grades earned, a graded certificate shall be issued to all the registered students after every semester. The grade certificate will display the course details (code, title, number of credits, grade secured) along with the SGPA of that semester and CGPA earned till that semester.

CHAPTER 2

RESEARCH APTITUDE

RESEARCH APTITUDE

Research: Meaning, Types, and Characteristics, Positivism and Post- positivistic approach to research.

Methods of Research: Experimental, Descriptive, Historical, Qualitative, and Quantitative methods.

Steps of Research.

Thesis and Article writing: Format and styles of referencing.

Application of ICT in research.

Research ethics.

The term 'Research' consists of two words: Research = Re + Search

'Re' means again and again and 'Search' means to find out something,

Characteristics of Research :

1. Empirical: Research is based on direct experience or observation by the researcher.

2. Logical: Research is based on valid procedures and principles.

3. Cyclical: Research is a cyclical process because it starts with a problem and ends with a problem.

4. Analytical: Research utilizes proven analytical procedures in gathering the data, whether historical, descriptive, experimental, or case study.

5. Critical: Research exhibits careful and precise judgment.

6. Methodical: Research is conducted in a methodical manner without bias using systematic methods and procedures.

7. Replicability: The Research design and procedures are replicated or repeated to enable the researcher to arrive at a valid and conclusive result 8. It is an intellectual inquiry or quest toward truth.

9. It leads to the enhancement of knowledge

10. Research refers to a series or systematic activities undertaken to find out the solution to a problem

11. Journey from known to unknown.

- **Ontology:** to inquire about the universe, the existence of god, matter, and after-death happenings are some of the questions
- **Epistemology**: its raining but to study why its raining

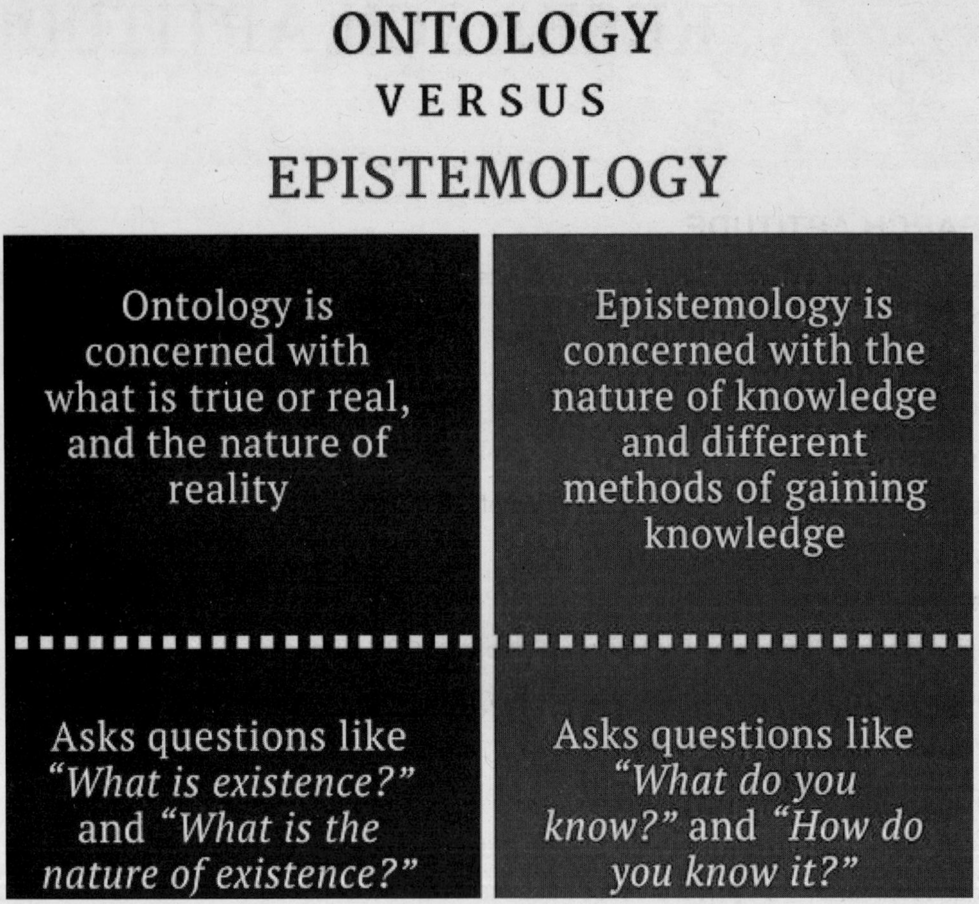

Positive paradigm:

- Factual knowledge gained through observation (senses and measurement) is trustworthy. Positivism depends on quantifiable observations that lead to statistical analyses.
- Positivism: There is a single reality which can be known. Every person will reach at the same result through the use of natural sciences (not considering researcher limitations)
- Post positivism: Reality can't be fully known. Efforts to understand reality are limited owing to human's sensory and intellectual limitations.

Characteristics	Positivist	Post-positivist
Data Type	Quantitative	Qualitative
Perspective	Objectivist	Subjectivist
Focus	Scientific	Humanistic
Methodology	Experimentalist	Interpretivist. The term interpretivism refers to epistemologies, or theories about how we can gain knowledge of the world, which loosely rely on interpreting or understanding the meanings that humans attach to their actions.
Use	Use to develop theory	Use to test theory

TYPES OF RESEARCH

1. Fundamental (basic or pure) Research:

The main purpose of basic research is to add to the existing stock of knowledge.

2. Applied Research

- Applied research is done to solve specific, practical questions facing society.
- It can be used for policy formulation, administration and understanding of a phenomena.

Fundamental research	Applied research
Addition to knowledge	Solution to existing problems
Discovery or invention	Innovation or application
Mostly academic	Practical use in solving a problem
Extensive in nature	Intensive in nature

3. Action Research:

- It is a part of applied research.
- Immediate solution of the problem.

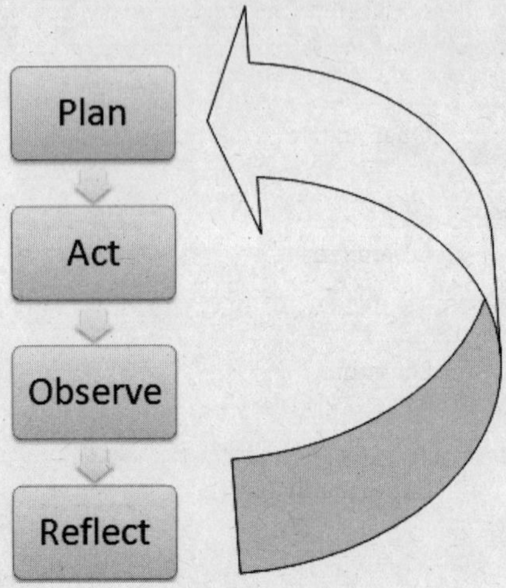

4. Exploratory Research: (unstructured)

- It is generally done at the beginning of a research.
- It is undertaken to explore an area where little is known or to investigate the possibilities of undertaking a particular research study.
- No need for a hypothesis as the problem is not defined.

5. Descriptive Research (structured) (aware of the problem but it is partially defined)

- Descriptive research is a quantitative research method. In simple words, descriptive research is all about describing the phenomenon, observing and drawing conclusions from it.
- No control over variables.
- Tells us what is?
- National Sample Surveys (NSS) and censuses can be taken as the best example of descriptive research.

6. Casual Research: highly structured

- Problem clearly define
- Tells us What will be
- Identify cause and effect relationship

7. Empirical Research:

It relies on experience and observation.

8. Ex-post facto Research: (non-experimental)

- It is conducted in the context of phenomena after it has occurred or at the time of occurrence.
- Independent variable is not manipulated.

9. Historical Research:

- It usually focuses on the historical aspects of an issue of interest or problem.
- Study the past-time to predict the future

- No manipulation or control over variables.
- Examples are the growth of trade unions in India, the evolution of the modern education system in India, etc.

10. Experimental Research:

- Experimental research is designed for establishing causal relationships.
- Independent variable is cause, it can be manipulated.
- Dependent variable is an effect, it can't be manipulated.
- Two groups are defined
- Control group: changes can't be made
- Experimental group: experiment/change is made.

Three characteristics of experimental research :

- Control
- Manipulation
- Observation

11. Quasi Experimental Research

- Random values can't be assigned to the group.
- Researcher does not have control over experiment.
- Experiment occurs in a natural setting.

True experiments:	Quasi-experiments:
Emphasize internal validity ▪ Assess cause & effect (in relatively artificial environment) ▪ Test clear, a priori hypotheses	**Emphasize external validity** ▪ Describe "real" / naturally occurring events ▪ Clear *or* exploratory hypotheses
Participants randomly assigned to exp. or control groups ▪ Participants & experimenter Blind to assignment	**Non-equivalent groups** ▪ Existing groups ▪ Non-random assignment ▪ Participants not blind ▪ Self-selection
Control study procedures ▪ Manipulate independent variable ▪ Control procedures & measures	**Full control may not be possible** ▪ May not be able to manipulate the independent variable ▪ Partial control of procedures & measures

12. Cross–sectional study:

one time interaction or one-timeata collection from multiple samples.

13. Longitudinal study:

A study that collects data more than once from the same individuals.

14. Quantitative research :

- It is similar to deductive research.
- It is also termed as linear research as it typically follows a linear path.
- Employ mathematical models
- Sample large
- Positivistic approach

15. Qualitative Research:

- It is inductive in nature, i.e., The research moves from specific to theory.
- In-depth understanding of human behavior
- Small but focused samples
- Post-positivistic approach

The important methods and approaches used in qualitative research:

- In-depth interview: one-to-one interview with one participant at a time.
- Focus group:6 to 10 participants who are subject matter experts.
- Narrative research: review literature
- Phenomenology: experience of a phenomena
- Ethnography: a study of cultures
- Case study research: study an organization or entity
- Content analysis: analyze social life
- Grounded theory: generate and develop theory

QUANTITATIVE RESEARCH VERSUS QUALITATIVE RESEARCH

Quantitative Research	Qualitative Research
Quantitative Research uses statistics	Qualitative Research uses descriptions and observations
Data can be measured accurately	Data can be observed and not measured
Considered to be objective	Considered to subjective
Uncovers measurable data to formulate theories and facts and uncover patterns	Helps to understand the underlying reasons, opinions, and motivations
Mainly uses hypotheses	Uses either hypotheses or research questions
Data collection methods are highly structured	Data collection methods are semi-structured or unstructured
The sample population is large	The sample population is small

QUALITATIVE DATA VERSUS QUANTITATIVE DATA

QUALITATIVE DATA	QUANTITATIVE DATA
Data type that consists of descriptive statements	Data type that can be measured and expressed numerically
Text-based	Number-based
Statistical analysis is harder	Statistical analysis is easier
Collected using interviews, written documents, observations	Collected using surveys, observations, experiments, and interviews

Structured approach:

- The structured approach to inquiry is usually classified as quantitative research.
- It is more appropriate to determine the extent of a problem, issue, or phenomenon by quantifying the variation. For example, how many people have a particular problem? How many people hold a particular attitude?

Unstructured approach

- The unstructured approach to inquiry is usually classified as qualitative research.
- It is more appropriate to explore the nature of a problem issue or phenomenon without quantifying it.

STEPS OF RESEARCH

Step 1

1. Formulation of Research Problem

Research problem is like an identification of a destination before undertaking a research journey.

2. Literature Review

3. Developing the objective: SMART

Specific – Measurable – Achievable – Relevant – Time Framed

4. Formulating a Hypothesis

Null Hypothesis (Ho): No difference

Alternative Hypothesis (Ha)

5. Preparing Research Design

6. Developing Data Collection Instrument

Primary data sources :

- Observations
- Experiments
- Questionnaire
- Personal Interview etc,

Questionnaire

1. Closed-ended questionnaire
2. Open-ended questionnaire
3. Combined questionnaire

Types of Observations:

1. Structured – for descriptive research
2. Unstructured – for exploratory research
3. Participant observation
4. Non-participant observation
5. DIsguIsed observation

Secondary data sources :

- Government Publications
- Journal Articles
- Websites, T.V., Radio
- Internal records, etc.

Objective and subjective data:

- Act-based, measurable, observable, and independent of any single person's opinion.
- Subjective data can be individuals' opinion.

Qualitative & Quantitative Data:

- Qualitative data without assigning numeric value.
- Quantitative data for statistical analysis.

7. Selecting Samples

- Sample Size: The larger the sample, the more is the accuracy.
- Methods of sampling from a population (Universe)

8. Collecting Data

9. Processing & Analyzing Data

10. Hypothesis Testing

Layout of the Research Report

A. Preliminary Pages
   A. Title and Date
   B. Acknowledgments
   C. Table of Contents
   D. List of Tables
B. Main Text
   A. Introduction
   B. Statement of Findings and Recommendations
   C. Results
   D. Implications of the Results
   E. Summary
C. End Matter
   A. Appendices
   B. Bibliography

Types of Variables:

1. Independent variable: Explanatory, predictor, regression, stimulus covariate control, exogenous.

2. Dependent variable: Explained, predicated, Regress, endogenous.

3. Intervening mediating: Establish a link between DV and IV.

4. Extraneous variable (like an independent variable): that factor that may affect the outcomes – we avoid that (these are not manipulated by the researchers)

5. Constant variables: only one value E.g., flower, tree.

6. Binary V / Dichotomous V: Two possible states (values) E.g., male, female.

7. Polytomous V: More than two categories E.g., below average, average, above the average.

Independent, dependent, and extraneous variables in a casual relationship.

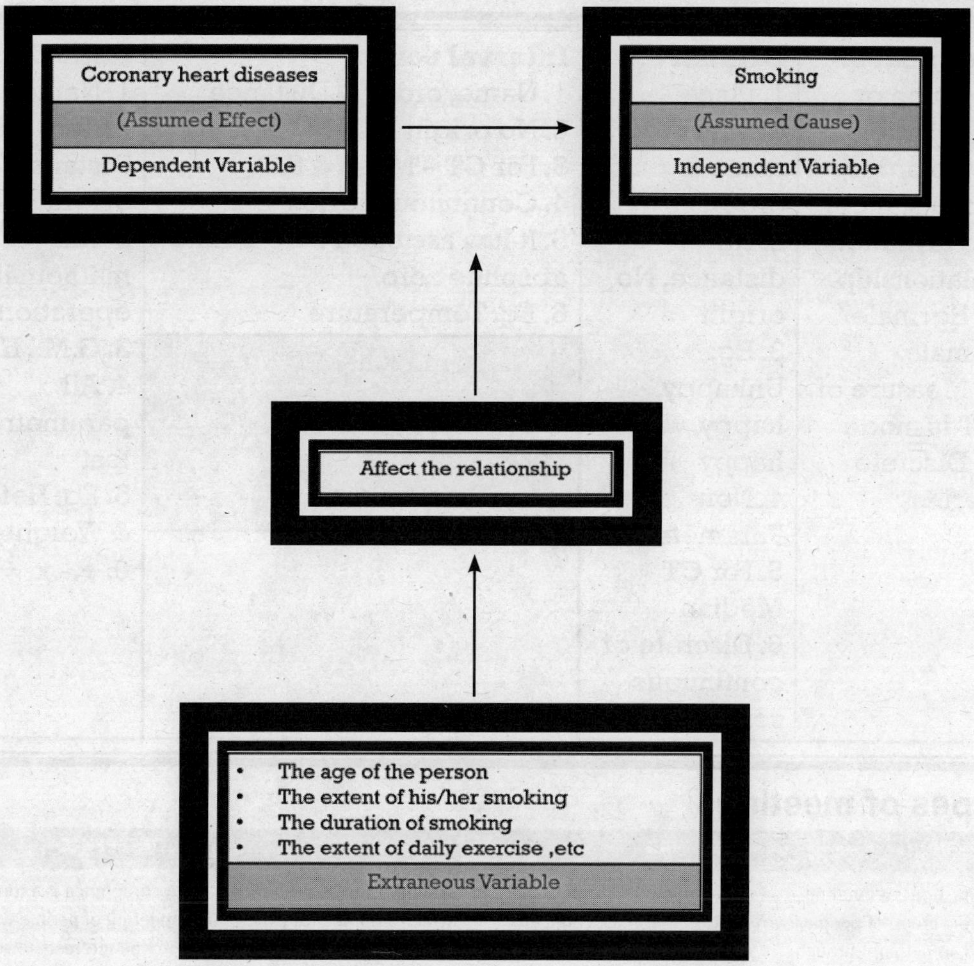

Measuring Variable: Types of scale

Scale Characteristics:

1. Description
2. Order
3. Distance
4. Origin

Nominal S.	Ordinal S.	Interval Series	Ratio S.
1. Name or categories 2. No order, No Distance, No arithmetic relationship 3. Eg: male/ female 4. Measure of CT is mode 5. Discrete Series	1. Place events in name & order. 2. No distance, No origin 3. Eg: Unhappy, happy, very happy 4. Non-Parametric T. 5. For CT Median 6. Discrete or continuous series	1. Name, order & Distance 2. No origin 3. For CT – Mean & S.D. 4. Continuous series 5. It has assumed zero but no absolute zero. 6. Eg: Temperature Waist, in inches 24 26 28 30 7. +, -	1. Name, order, Distance, origin 2. All mathematical operation. 3. G.M., H.M. 4. All parametric test 5. Eg: Height & Weight 6. +,-,x, ÷

Types of meetings

WORKSHOP	SEMINAR	SYMPOSIUM	CONFERENCE
A workshop is a meeting where a group of people learn about something through intensive discussions and activities related to it	A seminar is a form of academic instruction, either at an academic institution or organized by a professional organization	A symposium is a meeting at which a number of experts in a particular field discuss a particular subject	A conference is a formal meeting of people with shared interests, involving discussion, problem-solving. and consultation
Not very formal	Not very formal	Very formal	Formal
Tend to focus on a specific subject or topics	Can focus on more general topics	Tend to focus on a specific subject or topics	Can focus on more general topics
Offer more practical activities	Does not offer lot of practical activities	No practical activities	No practical activities
Can be one-day workshops or may continue for several days	Conducted in one day though they can be recurrent	Usually completed within one day	Can last for several days

Research Design

- **A research design** is a broad plan that states the objectives of the research project and provides guidelines on what is to be done to realize those objectives. It is, in other words, a master plan for executing a research project.

Types of Research Designs:

1. Exploratory Research Design: This design is followed to discover ideas and insights to generate possible explanations. It helps in exploring the problem or situation. It is, particularly, emphasized to break a broad vague problem statement into smaller pieces or sub-problem statements that help form a specific hypothesis.

- The exploratory research design is used to increase the familiarity of the analyst with a problem under investigation. This is particularly true when the researcher is new in the area, or when a problem is of a different type.

This design is followed to realize the following purposes:

1. Clarifying concepts and defining the problem.
2. Formulating the problem for a more precise investigation.
3. Increasing the researcher's familiarity with the problem
4. Developing hypotheses
5. Establishing priorities for further investigation

Exploratory research design is characterized by the flexibility to gain insights and develop hypotheses. It does not follow a planned questionnaire or sampling. It is based on a literature survey, experimental survey, and analysis of selected cases. Unstructured interviews are used to offer respondents a great deal of freedom. No research project is purely and solely based on this design. It is used as complementary to descriptive design and causal design.

2. Descriptive Research Design: Descriptive research design is typically concerned with describing the problem and its solution. It is a more specific and purposive study. Before rigorous attempts are made for descriptive study, a well-defined problem must be on hand. A descriptive study rests on one or more hypotheses.

For example, "Our brand is not much familiar," "Sales volume is stable," etc. It is more precise and specific. Unlike exploratory research, it is not flexible. Descriptive research requires clear specifications of who, why, what, when, where, and how of the research. Descriptive design is directed to answer these problems

3. Causal or Experimental Research Design: Causal research design deals with determining cause and effect relationships. It is typically in the form of an experiment. In causal research design, an attempt is made to measure the impact of manipulation on independent variables (like price, products, advertising, and selling efforts, or marketing strategies in general) on dependent variables (like sales volume, profits, brand image, and brand loyalty). It has more practical value in resolving marketing problems. We can set and test hypotheses by conducting experiments.

- Test marketing is the most suitable example of experimental marketing in which the independent variable like price, product, promotional efforts, etc., are manipulated (changed) to measure its impact on the dependent variables, such as sales, profits, brand loyalty, competitive strengths product differentiation and so on.

What is Reliability?

- Reliability refers to the consistency of the measurement. Reliability shows how trustworthy is the score of the test. If the collected data shows the same results after being tested using various methods and sample groups, the information is reliable. If your method has reliability, the results will be valid.
- Example: If you weigh yourself on a weighing scale throughout the day, you'll get the same results. These are considered reliable results obtained through repeated measures.
- Example: If a teacher conducts the same math test of students and repeats it next week with the same questions. If she gets the same score, then the reliability of the test is high.

What is the Validity?

- Validity refers to the accuracy of the measurement. Validity shows how a specific test is suitable for a particular situation. If the results are accurate according to the researcher's situation, explanation, and prediction, then the research is valid.
- If the method of measuring is accurate, then it'll produce accurate results. If a method is reliable, then it's valid. In contrast, if a method is not reliable, it's not valid.
- Example: Your weighing scale shows different results each time you weigh yourself within a day even after handling it carefully, and weighing before and after meals. Your weighing machine might be malfunctioning. It means your method had low reliability. Hence you are getting inaccurate or inconsistent results that are not valid.
- Most of the time, validity is difficult to measure even though the process of measurement is reliable. Example: If the weighing scale shows the same result, let's say 70 kg each time, even if your actual weight is 55 kg, then it means the weighing scale is malfunctioning. However, it was showing consistent results, but it cannot be considered as reliable. It means the method has low reliability.

Types of Reliability

Type of reliability	What does it measure?	Example
Test-Retests	It measures the consistency of the results at different points of time. It identifies whether the results are the same after repeated measures.	Suppose a questionnaire is distributed among a group of people to check the quality of a skincare product and repeated the same questionnaire with many groups. If you get the same response from a various group of participants, it means the validity of the questionnaire and product is high as it has high test-retest reliability.
Inter-Rater	It measures the consistency of the results at the same time by different raters (researchers)	Suppose five researchers measure the academic performance of the same student by incorporating various questions from all the academic subjects and submit various results. It shows that the questionnaire has low inter-rater reliability.
Parallel Forms	It measures Equivalence. It includes different forms of the same test performed on the same participants.	Suppose the same researcher conducts the two different forms of tests on the same topic and the same students. The tests could be written and oral tests on the same topic. If results are the same, then the parallel-forms reliability of the test is high; otherwise, it'll be low if the results are different
Inter-Term	It measures the consistency of the measurement.	The results of the same tests are split into two halves and compared with each other. If there is a lot of difference in results, then the inter-term reliability of the test is low.

Types of Validity

Type of valiidity	What does it measure?	Example
Content validity	It shows whether all the aspects of the test/measurement are covered.	A language test is designed to measure the writing and reading skills, listening, and speaking skills. It indicates that a test has high content validity.
Face validity	It is about the validity of the appearance of a test or procedure of the test.	The type of questions included in the question paper, time, and marks allotted. The number of questions and their categories. Is it a good question paper to measure the academic performance of students?
Construct validity	It shows whether the test is measuring the correct construct (ability/attribute, trait, skill)	Is the test conducted to measure communication skills is actually measuring communication skills?
Criterion validity	It shows whether the test scores obtained are similar to other measures of the same concept.	The results obtained from a prefinal exam of graduate accurately predict the results of the later final exam. It shows that the test has high criterion validity.

REFERENCE STYLES

APA Style	MLA Style
Used in social science	Used in humanities.
The title is in Italics – only the most necessary words are put in capital letters.	The title is underlined, all major words are capitalized.
The source page is titled as 'references' or reference link.	Source page is titled as 'works cited'
Here, only the last name of author is used.	Here, it is the full name.
Author's name and year of publication is used for 'in-text' citations.	Here, it is author's name and page numbers.
Commas are used for 'in-text' citations	No use of commas.

Abbreviation	Full Name
ACS	American Chemical Society
AGLC	Australian Guide to Legal Citation
AMA	American Medical Association
AMJ	Academy of Management style
Chicago	Chicago Manual of style
CSE (CBE)	Council of Science Editors/Council of Biology Editors

- **Shodhganga and Shodhgangotri**: Shodhganga is the name coined to denote the digital repository of Indian electronics thesis and dissertation set up by the Information and Library Network (INFLIBNET) Centre, of the University Grants Commission. Now, the candidates will have to store the thesis in a compact disc (CD) and upload each chapter in a separate PDF file using the naming convention as prescribed by Shodhganga.
- The CD must be authenticated by the Supervisor/ Head of Department.
- INFLIBNET introduced Shodhgangotri, which has been built to maintain a database of sypnosis of ongoing M.Phil./Ph.D. in Indian universities and institutions.

Plagiarism :

- Plagiarism is the representation of another person's thoughts, ideas, figures, or data, as one's own or incorporating someone else works into one's own without giving appropriate credit or citation to the original work.

Fabrication

- It refers to the intentional misrepresentation of research by making up data or results without performing the actual research.
- Falsification
- It refers to the manipulation of the research process, tempering/omission of data or results intentional manipulation of images or data representation in order to achieve desired results, or drawing misleading conclusions.
- At the time of Report writing and Report Submitting and Data collection, Research ethics is necessary.
- If pattern change of research, i.e. in the thesis, there is no negative effect on ethical value

Software used in plagiarism

- Viper, Quetext, Ithenticate, Turnitin (for an institution)

Software used in Statistics:

- SPSS (Statistical Package for social-science)
- SAS (Statistical Analysis System)
- Reference Management Software

HYPOTHESIS

Possible Hypothesis Test Outcomes		
	Actual Situation	
Decision	H0 True	H0 False
Accept H0	No error	Type II error
	Probability = 1 - α	Probability = β
Reject H0	Type I error	No error
	Probability = α	Probability = 1 - β

Types of Errors

- Type I – Hypothesis is true, but our test rejects it.
- Type II – Hypothesis is false, but our test accepts it.
- Level of Significance - The maximum size of Type I error, which we are ready to risk is called as the level of significance. It can be 5% or 1 %. If we fix the 5% level, it means we are 95% confident that our decision to reject the null hypothesis is true.
- Power of Test – The probability of committing Type II error is denoted by β. The power of the test is defined as the value '1-β'. Our aim is to fix the level of significance at 'α' and then maximize '1-β'.
- Null Hypothesis: It assumes that there is no difference between population parameters and sample statistics.
- Alternative Hypothesis: Alternative Hypothesis is accepted when the null hypothesis is rejected. It can be two-tailed, right-tailed, or left-tailed.

Hypothesis Testing

Small Sample Tests:

- T-test: developed by William Gosset.
- Applicable where the sample is less than 30.
- Degree of Freedom = n-1
- T-test is used to test the significance of the regression coefficient in the regression model.
- In multiple regression with 3 independent variables, the regression coefficient is to be tested by t-test.
- To test the hypothesis when the correlation coefficient in the population is Zero.
- Population variance is unknown as the sample size is small.
- Used for estimating the mean, and difference of means in independent and paired samples.

Large Sample Test:

1. Z-test: Given by Fisher.
2. If the coefficient correlation is not zero, then we use Z-test.

3. Used when the sample size is more than 30.
4. It is used to determine whether two population means are different.
5. Population variance is known as the sample size is large.
6. Used for estimating proportion, a difference of proportions, mean, and difference of means.
7. It is based on a standard normal distribution.
8. For each significance level, the z-test has a single critical value
9. At a 5% significance level for a two-tailed test, the z-value is 1.96. At a 1% significance level for two tailed test, it is 2.58

At 5% significance level, for one tailed test, it is 1.645 At 1% significance level for one tailed test, it is 2.33

$$Z_c = \frac{\overline{x} - \mu_0}{\sigma / \sqrt{n}}$$

Variance Ratio Test :

1. F -Test : Given by Fisher.
2. F -Test is used to the test two independent estimation of population variance.
3. Small sample test (Two sample $S_1{}^2$ and $S_2{}^2$ have same variance).
4. Variance Ratio $= \frac{S_1{}^2}{S_2{}^2}$
5. Degree of freedom for larger population variance is V1 and smaller is V2.
   V1=n-1 V2= n-2
6. F-tests are designed to test if two population variances are equal.
7. F-test never be -ve as the upper value is greater than the lower.
8. Testing of the overall significance of regression by F-test.
9. Test for the significance of the adjusted coefficient of multiple determination is the F-test.
10. Value of the F-test lies between 0 to ∞.

Chy Square Test

- Given by Karl Pearson.
- It is non- parametric test.

- Used to test the goodness of fit (r^2).
- Value lies between 0 to 1.
- Sample size must be greater than 50.
- For the contingency table having r rows and c columns, the test statistic follows chi-square distribution with (r-1)(c-1) degree of freedom provided

Parametric test	Non parametric test
Paired t- test	Wilcoxon Rank sum test
Unpaired test	Mann- Whitney U test
Pearson correlation	Spearman correlation
One way analysis of variance	Kruskal Wallis test

	Parametric test	Non-parametric test
1.	Used for ratio or interval data	For ordinal or nominal data
2.	Used for normal distribution	Any distribution
3.	Mean is usual central measure	Median is usual central measure
4.	Information about population is completely known	No information available
5.	Specific assumptions made regarding population	Assumption free test

Sampling

Census: census takes each item of the population and is considered tobe very authentic and reliable but it is time-consuming and costly.

Sampling is the collection of samples from out of the population. Larger thesample size, the more authentic is the sample.

Sampling method :

1. Probability / Random sampling

All units of the population have the same chance of being selected in thesample.

Simple unrestricted method: Techniques used are the lottery method,card technique, and tippet table.

Stratified sampling: The population is divided into different strata. Strata are defined in such a way that the population inside one strata ishomogeneous in nature and outside it is heterogeneous.

Systematic sampling: for e.g. I choose every 7th individual to be apart of my sample.

Multi-stage sampling: The sample is divided into stages.

Cluster sampling: Same as stratified sampling but under cluster sampling, clusters are heterogeneous inside and homogeneous outside.

2. Non- Probability Sampling

All items of population don't have same chance of being selected

- Judgment sampling
- Quota sampling
- Convenience sampling
- Snowball sampling

Stratified and Cluster Sampling

Stratified

- Population divided into few subgroups
- Homogeneity within subgroups
- Heterogeneity between subgroups
- Choice of elements from within each subgroup

Cluster

- Population divided into many subgroups
- Heterogeneity within subgroups
- Homogeneity between subgroups
- Random choice of subgroups

CHAPTER 3

COMPREHENSION

1. The RC section in the UGC NET exam evaluates candidates' ability to comprehend and interpret unseen passages.
2. This section comprises 5 questions, with each question carrying 2 marks, totaling 10 marks.

Reading Comprehension section, it is essential to focus on the following skills:

1. **Vocabulary**: Developing a strong command of vocabulary is crucial for comprehending passages effectively. Enhance your vocabulary by reading extensively, utilizing flashcards, and employing other vocabulary-building tools.
2. **Skimming and Scanning**: Skimming involves quickly reading through a passage to grasp its overall content while scanning involves searching for specific information. These skills enable you to identify key details swiftly and accurately and respond to questions.
3. **Analytical Thinking:** The ability to analyze passage information and draw logical conclusions is essential for answering questions that require drawing inferences or evaluating arguments.
4. **Time Management**: Efficient time management is critical since you have limited time to complete the Reading Comprehension section. Strive to finish each passage and its associated questions within the designated time limit.
5. **Practice**: Regular practice is key to improving your Reading Comprehension skills. Read a variety of texts, take practice tests, and analyze your mistakes to enhance your performance.

Ways to attempt RC:

1. Don't panic when you come across difficult words or complex language in the passage. Getting worried can make it harder to understand.
2. The first approach to tackle reading comprehension is to quickly go through the passage and then read a specific part again where the question is asked. This is especially helpful for beginners and reduces the chances of making mistakes. It also helps improve your reading skills and gives you a better overall understanding of the content.

3. The second approach is to first try answering the questions and then find the answers in the passage. In this method, you read and understand the question, and then look for similar words or phrases in the passage to find the section that has the answer. This approach is more suitable for people who are more

experienced, while beginners should follow the first approach.

Read the passage and answer the following:

The mechanism of commodification involves platforms transforming online and offline objects, activities, emotions, and ideas into tradable commodities. These commodities are valued through four different types of currency: attention, data, users, and money. Commodification is intensified by mechanisms of datafication as massive amounts of user data are collected and processed by online platforms.

This provides insight into the user's interests, preferences, and needs at particular moments in time. It also ties into mechanisms of selection as these users are connected with personalized services and advertisements. Commodification includes but does not equal, business models on a singular platform. Rather, the mechanism plays out in the multi-sided markets created through the platform ecosystem, which connects the infrastructural core with sectoral platforms.

Commodification mechanisms are simultaneously empowering and disempowering for users. The connector platforms allow individual users to market their assets or experiences online, be it their apartments, rides, eyewitness reports, or videos. They help commodity users' activities, enabling them to become entrepreneurs in their own right. On the other hand, the same platform mechanisms of commodification involve the exploitation of cultural labor, the labor of users, and on-demand service workers. Furthermore, these mechanisms lead to a concentration of economic power in the hands of a few platform owners and operators who act as aggregators and gatekeepers.

1. Commodities mechanism are:

   a. All powerful

   b. Data producers

   c. Legacy institutions

   d. Paradoxical instruments to users

The passage presents the different facets of:

   a. Online empowerment

   b. Online business models

   c. Sectoral Platforms

   d. Commodities in intangible assets

When ideas and emotions are converted into tradable commodities, it is a form of

   a. Transformational Trade

b. User preference

c. Commodification

d. Currency manipulation

When massive amounts of users' data are processed by the online platform, it is known as:

a. Personalised services

b. Selection Mechanism

c. Data ecosystem

d. Datafication

Commodification mechanism has its place in

a. Traditional business models

b. Multisided markets

c. Online Support Systems

d. Single commodity markets

Steps:

1. Read the question and target keywords.
2. Find that keyword or its synonyms in the passage.
3. For 1st question, target the last paragraph as the definition of commodification is clearly mentioned there.
4. For 2nd question, leave the lines that have been already read for the first question, focus on 1st paragraph as the main idea could be found there.
5. For 3rd question, we are already aware of similar terminologies we read in the first para.
6. Similarly, in the first para itself we can find the same keywords as question 4th is demanding.
7. Look at the options of the 5th question, we already read the 1st and last para multiple times. Now read the 2nd para, and there you can easily find the keyword multisided markets. Rest all options are not present in the passage.

The solution in detail for more understanding:

1. To solve this passage, first start by reading the passage. Now read the first question, as by reading this question we cannot directly find the linking words hence we have to find out the crux of the passage i.e., the passage says "Commodification mechanisms are simultaneously empowering and disempowering for users"., "On the other hand, the same platform mechanisms of commodification involve the exploitation of cultural labour, the labour of users, and on-demand service workers"., "They help commodity users' activities, enabling them to become entrepreneurs in their own right." From these

points we can conclude that answer (d) paradoxical instruments to users is correct.

2. Move on to the 2nd question, and read it, in the first paragraph itself, we can infer through the following lines that this is the **commodification of intangible assets**. "The mechanism of commodification involves platforms transforming online and offline objects, activities, emotions, and ideas into tradable commodities. These commodities are valued through four different types of currency: attention, data, users, and money." Hence option (d) is correct.
3. Look on to the 3rd question, this is the easiest question as from the first line itself we can find out the answer. "The mechanism of commodification involves platforms transforming online and offline objects, activities, emotions, and ideas into tradable commodities." Hence, it is a form of commodification.
4. "Commodification is intensified by mechanisms of datafication as massive amounts of user data are collected and processed by online platforms." when massive amounts of user data are processed by online platforms, it is known as datafication. From this statement, we can infer that datafication is the suitable option.
5. Refer to "Commodification includes, but does not equal, business models on a singular platform. Rather, the mechanism plays out in the multi-sided markets created through the platform ecosystem, which connects the infrastructural core with sectoral platforms." These lines convey that multisided markets are the correct option.

CHAPTER 4

COMMUNICATION

Communication

- Communication: Nature, characteristics, types, barriers and effective classroom communication
- Effective communication
- Mass-Media and Society

Types of communication

1. On the basis of media

Verbal

This involves the use of language and words for the purpose of passing on the intended message. In general terms, Verbal Communication means communication in the form of spoken words only. The verbal form may be oral or written as discussed below.

- **Written Communication:** This kind of communication involves any kind of exchange of information in the written form. For example, e-mails, texts, letters, reports, SMS, etc.
- **Oral Communication:** This verbal communication could be made on a channel that passes information in only one form i.e. sound.
- You could converse either face to face, or over the phone etc. This form of communication is an effective form.

Non-Verbal Communication

- In this type of communication, messages are relayed without the transmission of words. The messages here are wordless messages. This form of communication mainly aids verbal communication. It supplements it with gestures, body language, symbols, and expressions.

Some of the modes of non-verbal communication are:

Physical Non-verbal Communication

- Hand gestures, body language, facial expressions, the tone of one's voice, posture, touch, gaze, and others. For example, if you rest your head on your palms, it will mean that you are very disappointed or angry. Similarly, other subtle hints will convey your reaction to the presenter.

Kinesic communication

It is the technical term for body language, i.e., communicating by body movement.

Paralanguage

- The main kind of such communication is done with the tone of one's voice. Along with the tone of voice, the style of speaking, voice quality, stress, emotions serves the purpose of communication. And, these aspects are not verbal.

Aesthetic Communication

- Art is an important means of communication. Through the paintings or other forms of art, an artist can covey the strongest messages. Several times in the history of the world, art has been used as an effective form of nonverbal communication.

Appearance

- People will react to your appearance and this is a fact of life. Your clothes, the color of the fabrics, etc. all determine the reaction of your audience.

Visual Communication

- This is communication through visual aids like drawings, presentations, and illustrations, etc.

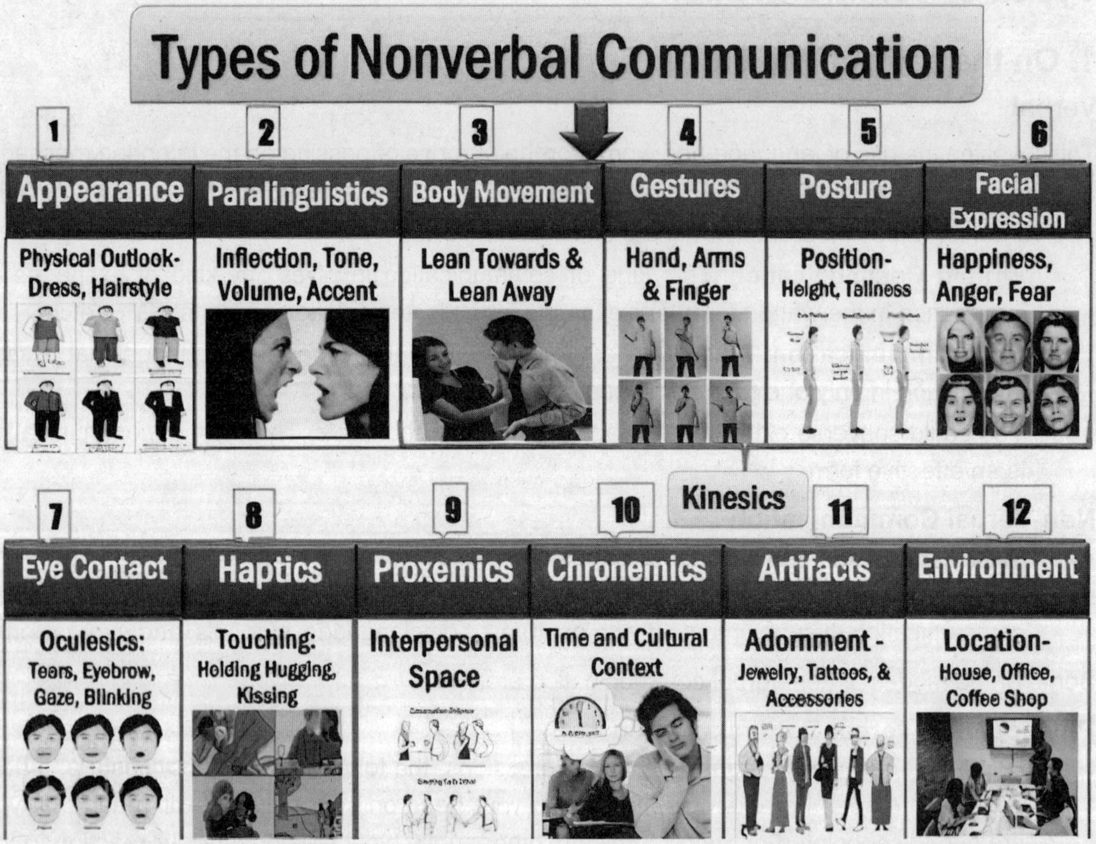

2. On the basis of relationship

Formal & Informal Communication

Formal communication refers to the flow of official information through proper, predefined channels and routes. In comparison, informal communication (grapevine) refers to communication which is multi-dimensional. Informal communication moves freely within the organization and is not bound by pre-defined channels and communication routes.

Difference between formal and informal communication

Basis	Formal communication	Informal communication
Mutual relationship among members	Based on formal superior-subordinate relationship.	Based on interpersonal contacts
Nature	Systematic and orderly.	Unsystematic and erratic.
Speed of communication	It is slow and time consuming.	It is fast and time saving.
Authenticity	Official and well planned messages are authentic.	Unofficial and un-planned messages may not be authentic.
Contents or subject matter	Work related matters, e.g. orders and instructions are communicated.	Personal matters are discussed.
Objectives	To achieve organi-sational objectives.	To meet personal needs and interests.

3. On the basis of flow or direction

- **Vertical:** The information or data flows up and down the organizational structure. **Downward communication**: from superior to subordinate like notices, circulars, orders. **Upward communication:** from subordinate to superior like opinions, ideas etc.
- **Horizontal (lateral):** This is the communication between two similar levels of the organization.
- **Diagonal:** This is the communication across the cross-functional levels of employees from various departments of the organization.

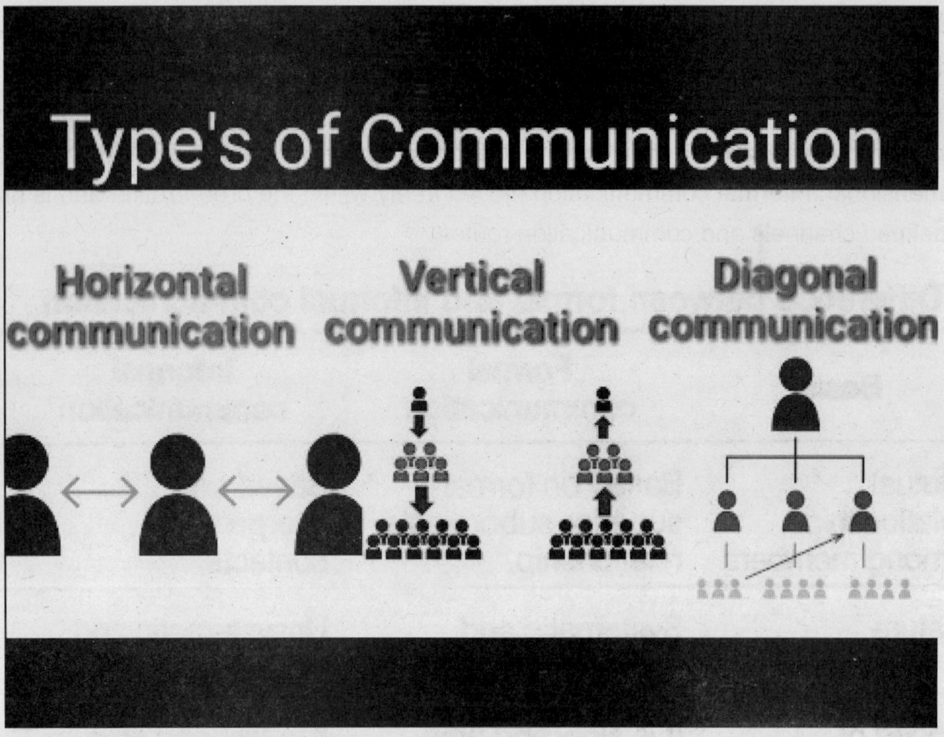

4. On the basis of participants

Intrapersonal: A man communicates with himself.

Interpersonal (dyadic) : A man communicates with other person .

Types of Interpersonal Communication

- One to One Communication - between only two people
- Group Discussion - 3 or more people, usually no more than 15
- Public Communication - one or more people speaking with a large audience; They are present with the audience
- Mass Communication - one or more people in front of a very large audience; not present with audience; always a medium, like TV, radio or internet

Communication style

Passive	Passive Aggressive	Aggressive	Assertive
Emotionally dishonest, indirect, inhibited, self-denying, blaming, apologetic.	*Emotionally dishonest, indirect. Self-denying at first. Self-enhancing at expense of others later.*	*Inappropriately honest, direct, expressive, attacking, blaming, controlling, self-enhancing at expense of others.*	*Appropriately honest, direct, self-enhancing, expressive, self-confident, empathic to emotions of all involved.*
"Others' rights and needs take precedence over mine"	*"I subtly make clear that my rights and needs prevail"*	*"I boldy insist that my rights and needs prevail"*	*I clearly express that we both have rights and needs"*

A Communication Model

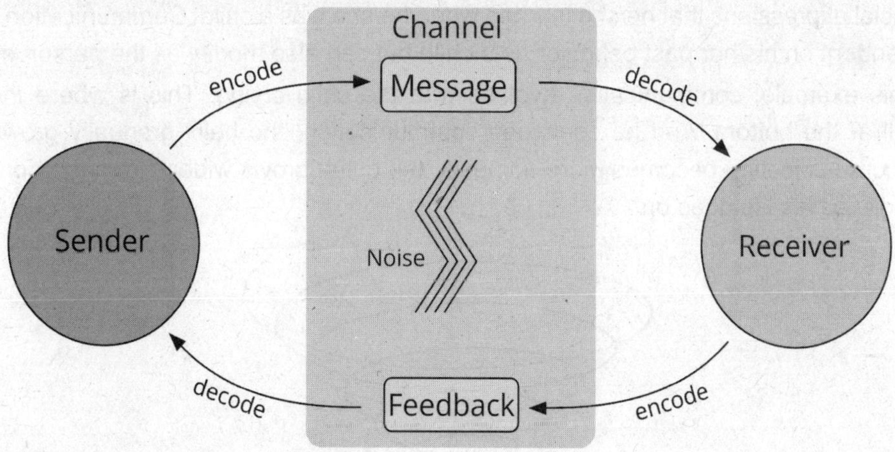

1. The Linear Communication Model

- It is straight-line communication found typically in mass communication; think television, radio, newspapers, etc. According to this model, there is no means for immediate feedback.
- Shannon and Weaver were the first to present the Linear Model of Communication in 1949's The Mathematical Theory of Communication.

2. Berlo's SMCR Model of Communication

- David Berlo's SMCR Model of Communication represents the process of communication in its simplest form. The acronym SMCR stands for Sender, Message, Channel, and Receiver.
- Berlo's SMCR Model of Communication (1960) describes the different components that form the basic process of communication. There is no feedback, no noice and no concept of barriers of communication.it is linear model of communication.

3. Helical model

Helical model of communication introduces the concept of time where continuousness of the communication process and relational interactions are very important. Communication is taken as a dynamic process in helical model of communication and it progresses with age as our experience and vocabulary increases.

- At first, helical spring is small at the bottom and grows bigger as the communication progresses. The same effect can be seen with communication of humans, where you know nothing about a person at first and the knowledge grows steadily as you know the person better. It considers all the activities of the person, from the past and present.
- Communication is supposed to be continuous and non-repetitive. It is always growing and accumulative. A child crying at birth signifies the communication of the child to its parents that he/she is alive. After some years, the child cries whenever the child needs anything like food or attention. He/she learns words and starts communicating with words.
- The child learns specific languages and communicates with the people who know the language that he/she knows. Communication becomes more complex as the child grows into adult and to the existing moment. The adult uses the same pronunciations and use of words or facial expressions that he/she learned when he/she was a child. Communication is directly dependent on his/her past behavior as a child but can also modify as the person grows.
- In this example, communication evolves with the child crying. This is where the helix is small at the bottom. And he continues communication, the helix gradually grows. When the communication becomes more complex, the spiral grows wider. From then on, it grows steadily as his life goes on.

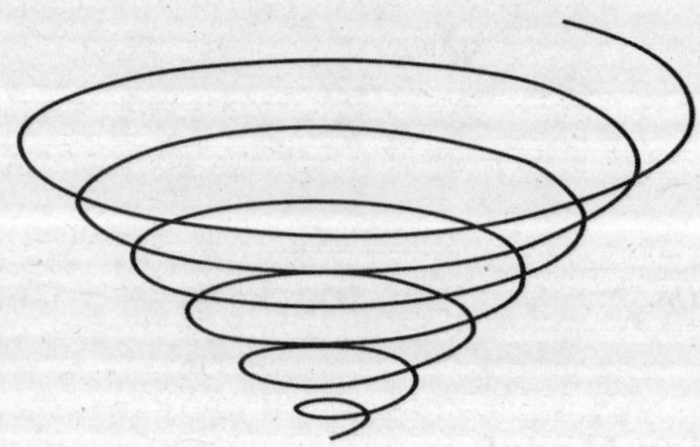

4. Transactional model

- **Transactional model** is the process of continuous change and transformation where every component is changing such as the people, their environments and the medium used. Due to this, it assumes the communicators to be independent and act any way they want.
- Since both sender and receiver are necessary to keep the communication alive in transactional

model, the communicators are also interdependent to each other. For example, transactional communication is not possible if the receiver is not listening to sender.

- The transactional model is the most general model of communication. Everyday talk and interactions are also a form of transactional model communication. It is more efficient for communicators with similar environment and individual aspects. For instance, communication between people who know each other is more efficient as they share same social system. Classroom communication is example of transactional communication.

5. Interactive model

Interactive model (also known as convergence model) deals with exchange of ideas and messages taking place both ways from sender to receiver and vice-versa.

- The communication process take place between humans or machines in both verbal or non-verbal way. This is a relatively new model of communication for new technologies like web.
- In Interactive model, whenever a source sends a message to a receiver (source), he/she encodes the message first. The encoded message is then received by the receiver where it is decoded to get the original information. Again, the receiver acts as a source, encodes another message (also knows as a feedback) and sends it back to the sender.

Difference:

In transactional model, Sender and receiver both play equally important role in communication. Non-verbal feedback like gestures, body language, is also considered as feedback in this model.

Interactive model is mostly used for new media like the internet. Here, learners can respond to any mass communications like videos, news, etc. learners can exchange their views and ideas.

Unlike the Interaction Model, which suggests that participants alternate positions as sender and receiver, the Transaction Model suggests that you are simultaneously a sender and receiver. For example, when you first meet a client, you send verbal messages saying hello, who you are, and why you are there.

Barriers to Communication

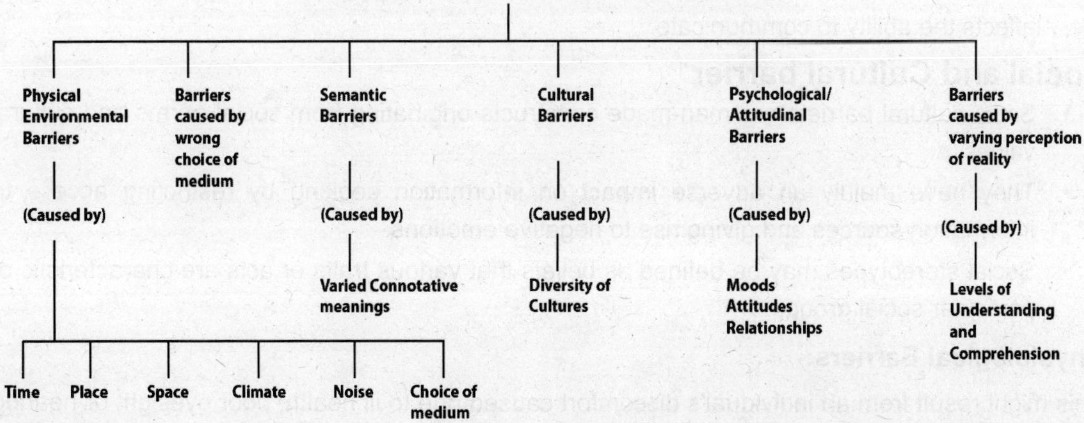

Physical barrier:

- A physical barrier is an environmental and natural condition that acts as a barrier in communication in sending a message from sender to receiver.
- Noise, an overload of information, an overabundance of information, distance, time, invisibility, ill-health, etc.
- When messages are sent by the sender, physical barriers like doors, walls, distance, etc. do not let the communication become effective. The barriers are less if the proximity of the sender and the receiver is high and fewer technologies are required.

Language barrier

A language barrier is a figurative phrase used primarily to refer to linguistic barriers to communication, i.e. the difficulties in communication experienced by people or groups originally speaking different languages, or even dialects in some cases.

Semantic Barriers:

It could arise due to differences in meanings that people attach to different words. Such as,

- Polysemy means there could be more than one meaning for a word or phrase. The use of such words can complicate the meaning and result in communication failure.
- Clichés are words and phrases that are overused and are no longer considered fresh or new. For example, the phrase they all lived happily ever after.

Technical barrier:

- Technology has helped reduce and even overcome distance, allowing people to share information without needing to meet in real life.
- But, there's more to physical barriers than distance.
- Physical barriers to digital communication include other environmental conditions like time, place, and medium.

Psychological barrier:

- • The Psychological or Emotional Barriers refer to the psychological state i.e. Opinions, attitudes, status consciousness, emotions, Pre-disposed notions, etc. of a person that deeply affects the ability to communicate.

Social and Cultural barrier

- Socio-cultural barriers are man-made constructs originating from social norms and cultural values.
- They have mainly an adverse impact on information seeking by restricting access to information sources and giving rise to negative emotions.
- Social stereotypes may be defined as beliefs that various traits or acts are characteristic of particular social groups.

Physiological Barriers:

This might result from an individual's discomfort caused due to ill health, poor eyesight or hearing issues, etc.

Important terms:

Effective communication : It is the process of exchanging ideas, thoughts, opinions, knowledge, and data so that the message is received and understood with clarity and purpose. When we communicate effectively, both the sender and receiver feel satisfied.

Entropy: refers to messages which convey highly unpredictable information to the receiver

Redundancy: refers to messages which convey highly predictable information to the receiver. If redundancy is too high (i.e. there are too many highly predictable messages) then this requires almost no effort to decode the messages, as there is little in the way of information that needs to be decoded.

Jargon is occupation-specific language used by people in a given profession, the "shorthand" that people in the same profession use to communicate with each other. For example, plumbers might use terms such as elbow, ABS, sweating the pipes, reducer, flapper, snake, and rough-in.

Ice breakers can be an effective way of starting a training session or team-building event. As interactive sessions run before the main proceedings, they help people get to know each other and buy into the purpose of the event. If such a session is well-designed and well-facilitated, it can really help get things off to a great start. By getting to know each other, getting to know the facilitators, and learning about the objectives of the event, people can become more engaged in the proceedings and so contribute more effectively towards a successful outcome. These sessions are designed to "break the ice" at an event or meeting. The technique is often used when people who do not usually work together, or may not know each other at all, meet for a specific, common purpose.

Consider using an ice breaker when:

- Participants come from different backgrounds.
- People need to bond quickly so as to work towards a common goal.
- Your team is newly formed.
- The topics you are discussing are new or unfamiliar to many people involved.
- As facilitator you need to get to know participants and have them know you better

Paraphrasing involves putting a passage from source material into your own words.

Summarizing involves putting the main idea into your own words, including only the main point.

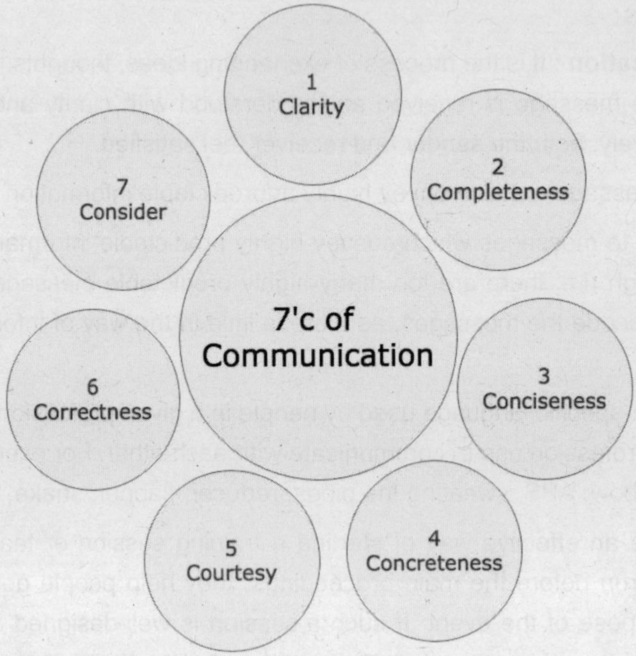

4 S's of Communication

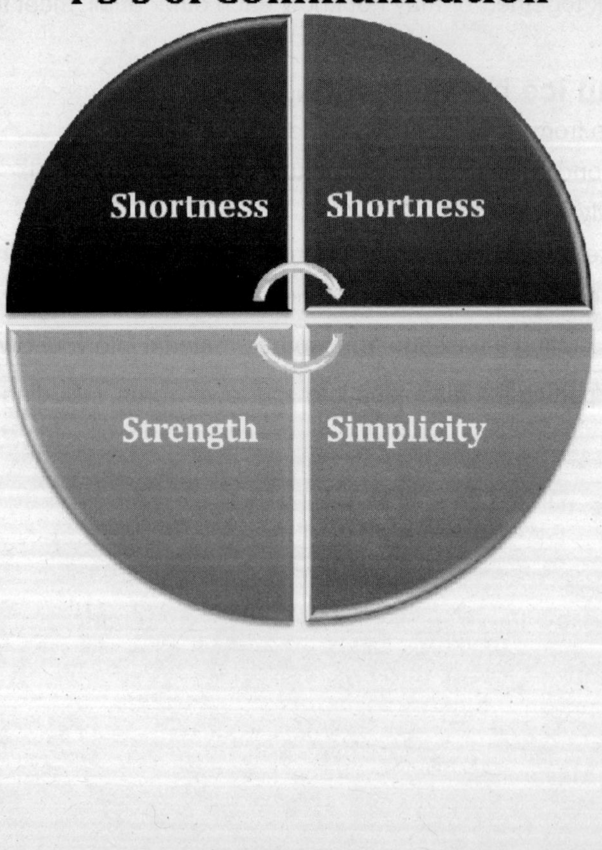

CHAPTER 5

MATHEMATICAL REASONING AND APTITUDE

Syllabus:

- Mathematical Reasoning - Number series, Letter series or Coding decoding, Blood Relations, Directions.
- Mathematical Aptitude Basic - Percentage, Fraction, Ratio & Proportion, Average
- Advanced Mathematical Aptitude: - Profit & loss, Discount, Time-speed-distance, Problems on trains, Simple & Compound Interest, Time & Work, Problems on Ages, Boat & streams.

Numbers:

- Natural Numbers: 1 to infinity
- Whole Numbers: 0 to infinity
- Real Numbers: Rational + irrational
- Integers: -infinity to +infinity
- Composite Numbers: These are not prime
- Prime Numbers: Whose factor is only 1 and the number itself.

Number Series: Important points

* There is no specific sequence formula by which a series is formed.
* If change in series is slow then it is a diffrence series. It is generally due to Addition or subtraction.
* If the change is initially sharp but later slow, then it is due to addition of squared or cubed terms.
* If the number series is alternating, then it may be a mixed series with two operations going on alternately

Number Series:

1. **Prime Number Series:**

   7, 11, 13, 17, 19, __?

   Solution: 7, 11, 13, 17, 19, 23.

   Here we had just picked up the next prime number after 19. There are a total of 25 prime numbers to 100.

   3, 7, 17, 31, __?

   Solution: 3, 5, 7, 11, 13, 17, 19, 23, 29, 31, 37, 41, 43, 47, 53.

   In this question, we first skipped 5(i.e., only one prime number) then skipped 11 and 13(two prime numbers, similarly we followed the pattern by skipping 3 prime numbers and then 4 prime numbers after 31. Hence, the answer is 53.)

2. **Addition Series: (difference increases slowly)**

   2, 8, 14, 20, __?

   Solution: 2+6=8, 8+6=14, 14+6=20, 20+6=26.

3. **Difference Series: (difference decreases slowly)**

   200, 192, 184, 176, __?

   Solution: 200-8=192, 192-8= 184, 184-8= 176, 176-8=**168.**

4. **Multiplication Series: (difference increases rapidly)**

   6, 24, 96, 384, __?

   Solution: 6x4=24, 24x4=96, 96x4=384, 384x4=**1536**.

5. **Division Series: (difference decreases rapidly)**

   4500, 900, 180, 36, __?

   Solution: 4500/5=900, 900/5=180, 180/5=36, 36/5=**7.2**

6. **N^2 Series:**

   1, 4, 9, 16, 25, __?

   Solution: 1^2=1, 2^2=4, 3^2=9, 4^2=16, 5^2=25, 6^2=**36.**

7. **N^2+1 Series**:

   10, 17, 26, 37, 50, __?

   Solution: 3^2+1=10, 4^2+1=17, 5^2+1=26, 6^2+1=37, 7^2+1=50, 8^2+1=**65.**

8. **N^2+N Series:**

   20, 30, 42, 56, __?

   Solution: 4^2+4=20, 5^2+5=30, 6^2+6=42, 7^2+7=56, 8^2+8=**72.**

9. N^2-1 Series:

224, 195, 168, 143, __?

Solution: $15^2-1=224$, $14^2-1=195$, $13^2-1=168$, $12^2-1=143$, $11^2-1=$**120**.

10. N^2-N Series:

210, 240, 272, 306, __?

Solution: : $15^2-15=210$, $16^2-16=240$, $17^2-17=272$, $18^2-18=306$, $19^2-19=$**342**.

11. Alternate Series:

15, 14, 19, 11, 23, 8, __?

Solution: In this series, alternate numbers have to be observed. Like 15+4=19, 14-3=11, 19+4=23, 11-3=8, 23+4= **27**. Number 3 is deducted from 14 and 11 whereas number 4 is added to 15, 19, and 23.

Letter Series or Coding-Decoding:

ALPHABET	NUMBER	OPPOSITE	TRICK	ALPHABET	NUMBER	OPPOSITE
A	1	Z	AZad	N	14	M
B	2	Y	BoY	O	15	L
C	3	X	CraX	P	16	K
D	4	W	DeW	Q	17	J
E	5	V	EVen	R	18	I
F	6	U	FUll	S	19	H
G	7	T	GifT	T	20	G
H	8	S	High School	U	21	F
I	9	R	Indian Railway	V	22	E
J	10	Q	Joker and Queen	W	23	D
K	11	P	PicK	X	24	C
L	12	O	LOve	Y	25	B

Trick: Remember the word EJOTY. E=5, J=10, O=15, T=20, Y=25. Now you know the 5 alphabet corresponding numbers, you can recall the alphabet preceding and following the EJOTY (table of 5) alphabet.

1. If KOLKATA is coded as LPMLBUB, then MUMBAI will be coded as:

Solution: KOLKATA similarly MUMBAI

+1↓ +1↓

LPMLBUB NVNCBJ

2. If ELEPHANT is coded as SMZGODHD, then TIGER will be coded as:

Solution: Reverse and -1

ELEPHANT TIGER

-1 -1

SMZGODKD QDFHS

3. If BIHAR is coded as 38, then GOA will be coded as:

Solution: BIHAR=2+9+8+1+18=38, GOA=7+15+1=23

4. If SMILE PLEASE is coded as IPA, IPA, IPA, then VERY SMART will be coded as:

Solution: Repetition

smIle PleAse=repetition of 3rd alphabet, IPA, IPA, IPA. Hence VERY SMART will be coded as veRy sMarT i.e., RMT, RMT, RMT.

5. If DIAMOND is coded as WRZNLMW, then PLATINUM will be coded as:

Solution: Opposite alphabet

DIAMOND PLATINUM

↓ ↓

WRZNLMW KOZGMFN

Blood Relations:

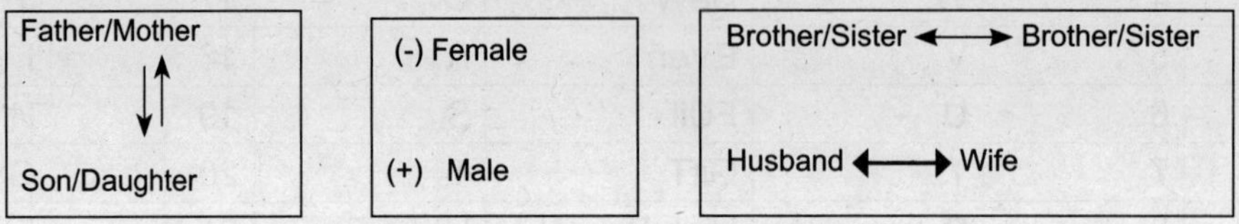

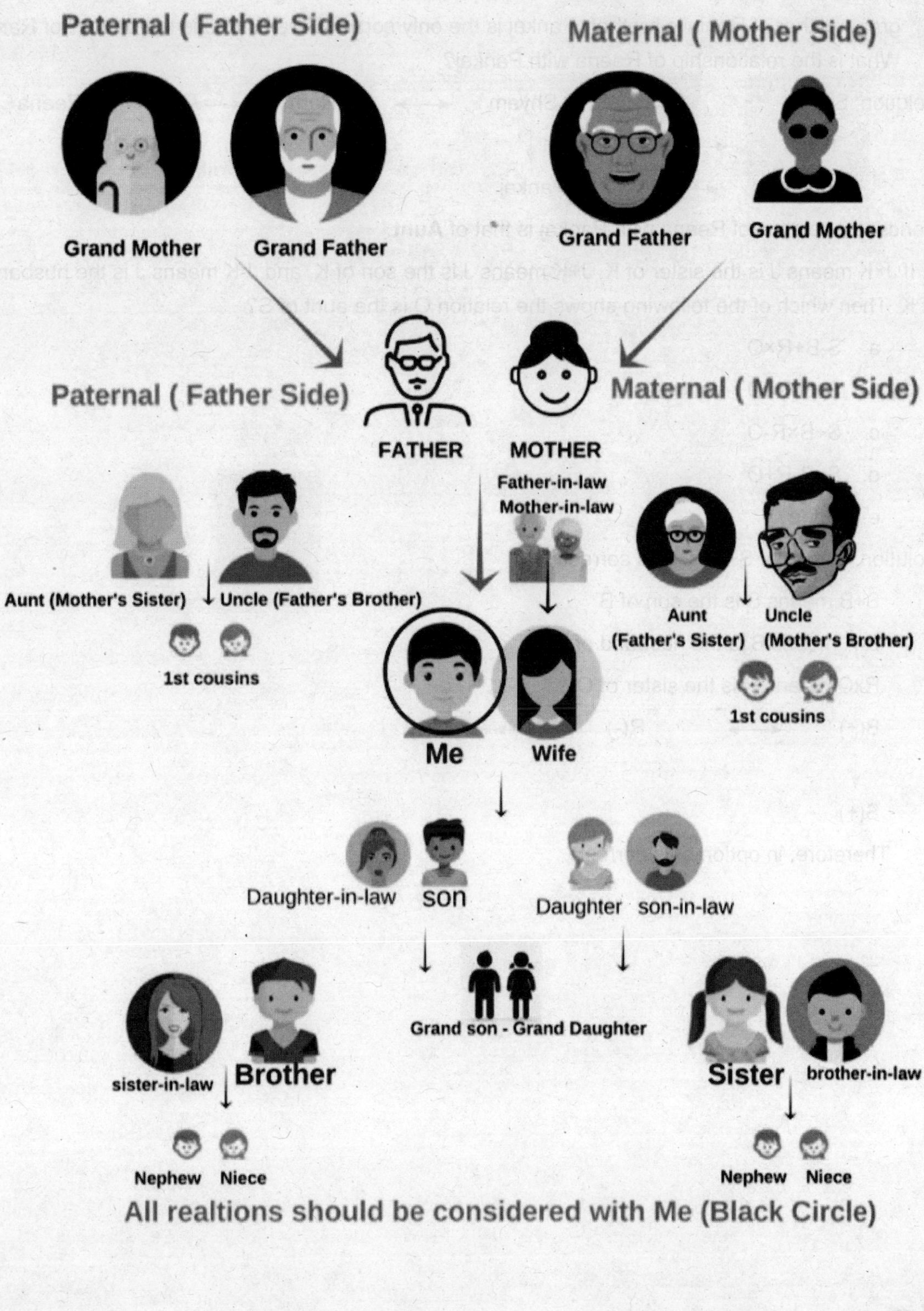

All realtions should be considered with Me (Black Circle)

1. Ram, Reena, Shyam, Pankaj, Rohini, and Sita are six family members. Ram and Reena are a married couple. Rohini is sister of Pankaj. Reena is the daughter-in-law of Sita, who is the grandmother of Rohini's brother. Pankaj is the only son of Shyam, who is the brother of Ram. What is the relationship of Reena with Pankaj?

Solution: Sita Shyam ⟷ Ram ⟷ Reena

Ram ⟷ Reena ↓

Rohini ⟷ Pankaj

Hence, the relation of Reena with Pankaj is that of **Aunt**.

2. If J×K means J is the sister of K, J+K means J is the son of K, and J-K means J is the husband of K. Then which of the following shows the relation O is the aunt of S?

a. S-B+R×O
b. S+B-R×O
c. S+B×R-O
d. S×B-R+O
e. None

Solution: Option b. S+B-RxO is correct.

S+B means S is the son of B

B-R means B is the husband of R

RxO means R is the sister of O

B(+) ⟷ R(-) ⟷ O(-)

↓

S(+)

Therefore, in option b. is correct.

Directions:

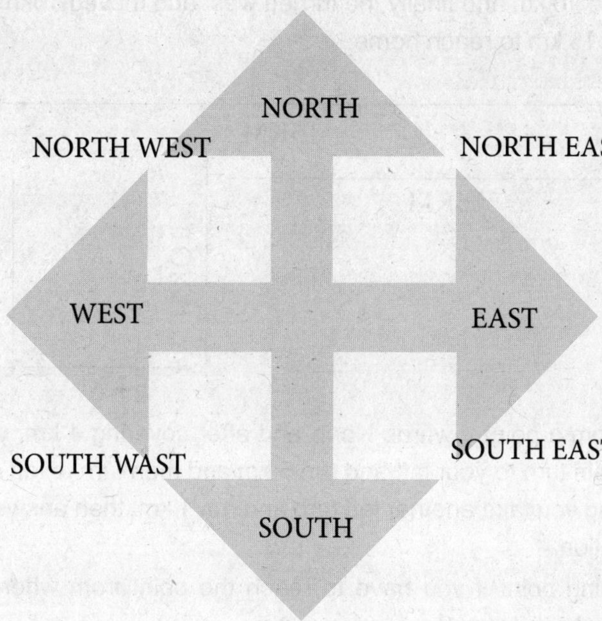

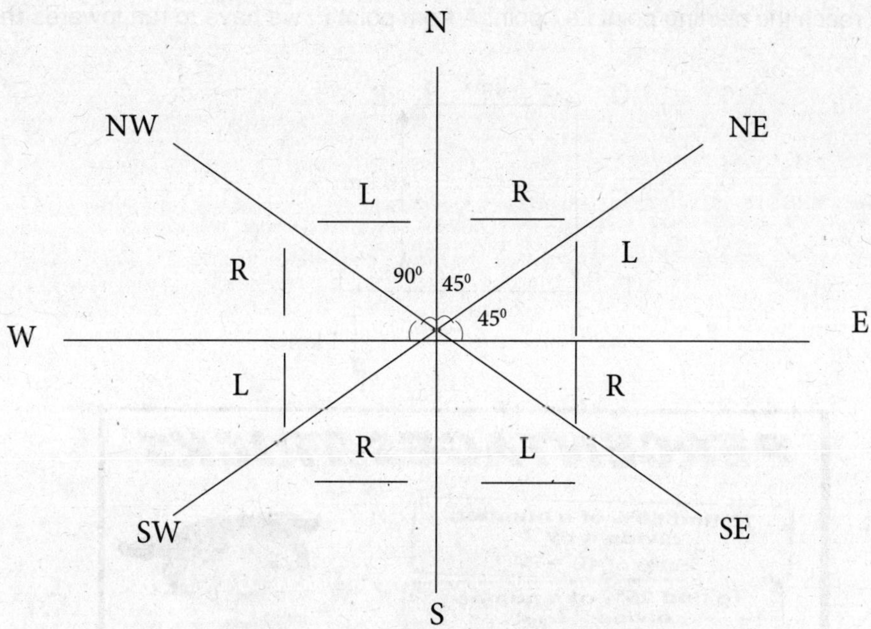

One day Ravi left home and cycled 10 km southwards, turned right and cycled 5 km and turned right and cycled 10 km, and turned left and cycled 10 km. How many kilometres will he have to cycle to reach his home straight?

- **Solution**: To calculate the distance from point B to point A. He has to travel a total of 15km from point B to A to reach back home. He started from point A and travelled in the south direction, turned towards the west (his right) and moved 5km, again turned towards the north and moved 10 km and finally, he turned west and moved 10km to point B. Hence, total distance will be 15 km to reach home.

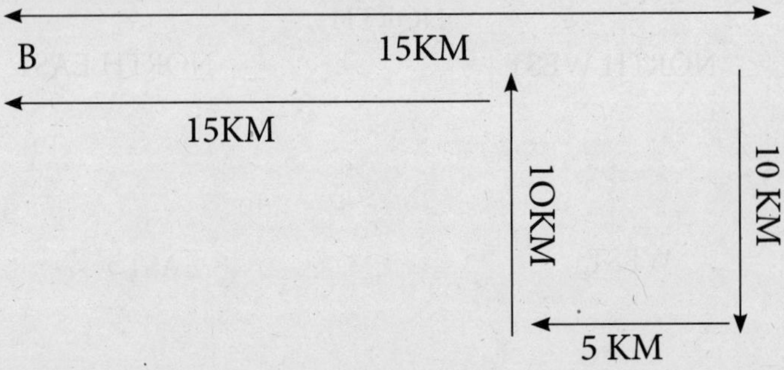

If you start running from a point towards North and after covering 4 km, you turn to your left and run 5 km and then again turn to your left and run 5 km and then turn to left again and run another 6 km and before finishing you take another left turn and run 1 km, then answer the following question based on this information.

- From the finishing point if you have to reach the point from where you started, in which direction will you have to run?

Solution: To reach the starting point i.e., point A from point F, we have to run towards **the West.**

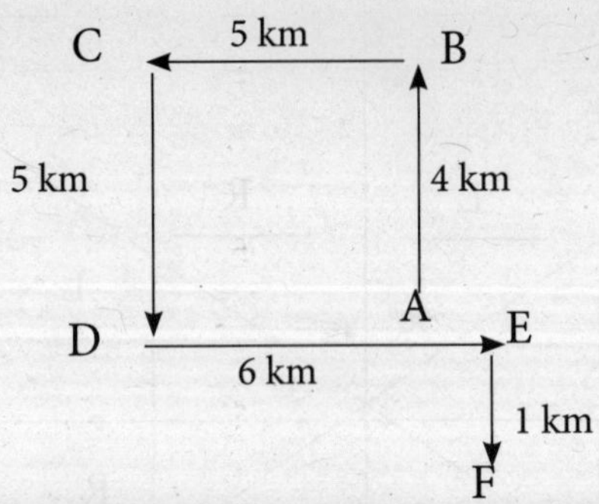

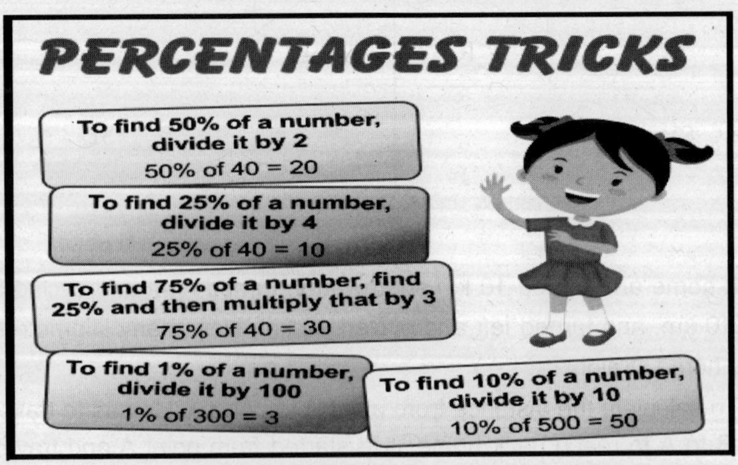

Mathematics

Percentage

1. A% of B = B% of A.
2. % increase $= \dfrac{\textit{increase value} - \textit{original value} \times 100}{\textit{Original value}}$
3. % decrease $= \dfrac{\textit{Original value} - \textit{decreased value} \times 100}{\textit{Original value}}$

Percentage	Fraction
100%	1/1
50%	1/2
25%	1/4
12.5%	1/8
6.25%	1/16
33.33%	1/3
16.66%	1/6
11.11%	1/9
18.18%	1/11
80%	4/5
60%	3/5
40%	2/5
20%	1/5
10%	1/10
14.28%	1/7
8.4%	1/12

4. Practice Questions with Solutions:

a. 450% of 16

400% of 16 + 50% of 16

16x4 + 8 = 72.

b. 36% of 225

30% of 225 + 6% of 225

67.5 + 13.5 = 81.

c. 77.77% of 2124

7/9 x 2124 = 1652.

d. Yash scores 175 marks and failed by 35 marks. If the passing % of the test is 35%. Find maximum marks?

- **Solution**: Yash scored 175 marks and failed by 35 marks. Hence passing marks are (175+35 = 210), which is equal to 35%.

35% = 210

1% = 210 x 1/35

Maximum marks will be: 210 x 100/35 = **600**.

e. What percent of 40 is 10?

x/100 x 40 = 10

x=25%

f. A fruit seller had some oranges, he sells 30% oranges and still have 140 oranges. Find how many oranges he had?

Given that 30% oranges are sold, hence 70% are left.

70% = 140

100% = 140/70 x 100

= **200 Oranges.**

g. Aditya has some amount of which 25% is stolen. 10% he gave to his friend and 50% of remaining is spend in a party. Rest 26 he gave to his mother. Find initial amount?

Let Aditya has Rs. 100 initially.

25 is stolen so 100-25=75, 10 he gave to his friend so 75-10=65, 50% of 65 he spent in a party i.e., 65/2 = 32.5

As per question he is left with Rs. 26 which is equal to 32.5%.

Therefore, 32.5% = 26

100% = 26/32.5 x 100 = 80 Rs

Aditya has Rs 80 initially.

h. Kartik earns Rs. 400 per week from his part-time job. He is to be given a 5% pay rise. How much will he earn?

Initial salary = 400

Increased salary = 5% of 400 = 20

New Salary = 400+20 = **420** Rs.

i. The price of all toys in a shop is to be increased by 8%. Calculate the new price of toys that originally cost Rs. 150.

Original price of toys = 150

Increased Price = 100+8% of 150 = 1.08 x 150 = **162** Rs.

j. **The population of the town was 48600. It increased by 25% in the first year and decreased by 8% in the second year. What will be the population of the town at the end of two years?**

Increase in the first year = 25% of 48600 = 12150

The population at the end of the first year = 12150+48600 = 60750

Decrease in the second year = 8% of 60750 = 4860

The population at the end of the second year = 60750 – 4860 = **55890.**

OR

Population at the end of first year = 48600 x 125/100 = 60750

Population at the end of second year = 60750 x 92/100 = 55890.

Percentage (Price and Consumption)

1. If the Price of the commodity increases by R% then the reduction in consumption so as not to increase the expenditure will be:

$$\left(\frac{R X 100 \%}{R+100}\right)$$

2. If the Price of the commodity decrease by R% then the increase in consumption so as not to decrease the expenditure will be:

$$\left(\frac{R X 100 \%}{100+R}\right)$$

3. Example: If the price of rice decreases by 25%, then by what % its consumption should be increased so that there is no change in expenditure?

$$\left(\frac{R X 100}{100-R}\right)=\left(\frac{25 X 100}{100-25}\right)$$

$$\frac{25}{75}\times 100\%=33.33\%$$

Fraction

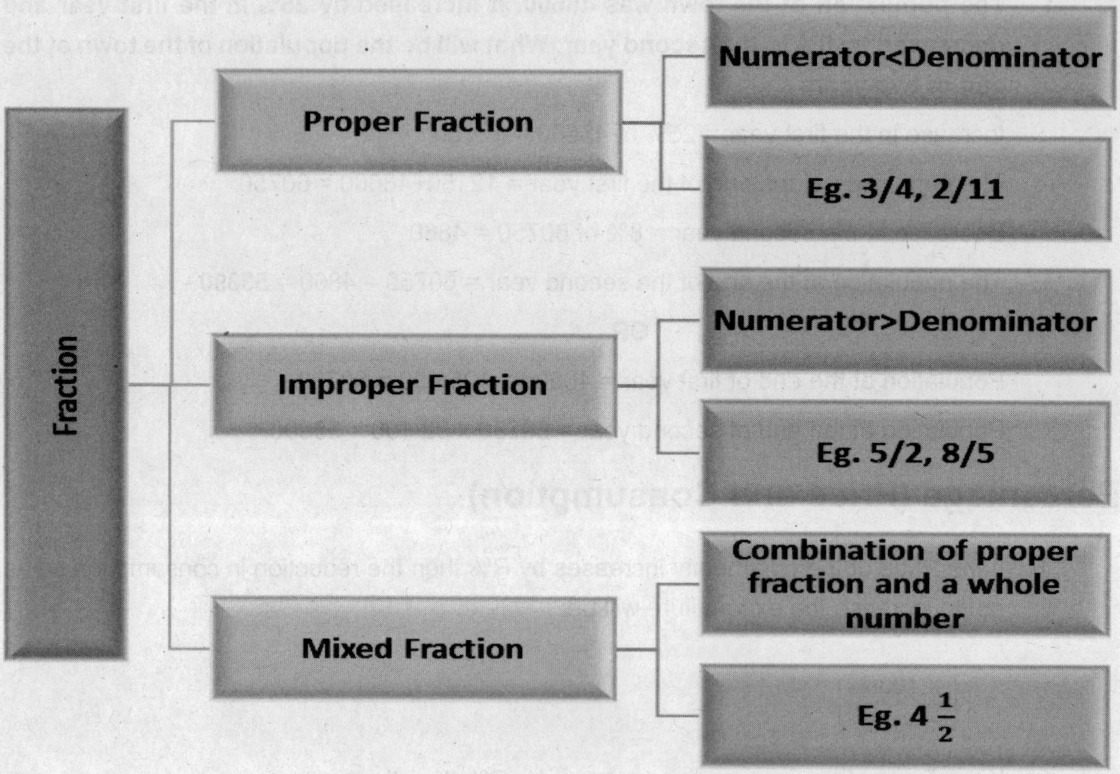

Conversion:

1. Mixed fraction to improper fraction:

   $4\frac{2}{5}$ = 4x5+2 = 22/5

2. Improper fraction to mixed fraction:

   22/5 = 4 is the quotient and 2 is the reminder. Hence, $4\frac{2}{5}$ is the mixed fraction

3. Solve $12\frac{1}{3} + 4\frac{3}{4} + 5\frac{1}{3}$

   First add all the whole numbers = 12+4+5 = 21

4. Now, add fractions = $21 + \frac{1}{3} + \frac{3}{4} + \frac{1}{3}$

   $= 21 + \frac{1X4+3X3+1X4}{12}$

   $= 21 + \frac{17}{12}$

   $= 21 \text{ X } \frac{12}{12} + \frac{17}{12}$

   = 252 + 17/12

= 269/12

$=22\frac{5}{12}$

Ratio and Proportion

1. A:B :: C:D or B:A :: D:C
2. A/B = C/D or B/A = D/C
3. A C

B D

A X D = B X C

4. A:B :: C:D, here A and D are extreme terms and B and C are mean terms.
5. A:B, here A is antecedent and B is consequent.
6. Duplicate Ratio: A:B = A^2:B^2
7. Sub-Duplicate Ratio: A:B = $\sqrt{A}: \sqrt{B}$
8. Triplicate Ratio: A:B = A^3:B^3
9. Sub-Triplicate Ratio: A:B = $\sqrt[3]{A}: \sqrt[3]{B}$

Questions for Practice with Solution: -

1. Out of the total students in the class, if number of boys is 5 and number of girls is 3. Then ratio between girls and boys is?

   The ratio of girls: boys is 3:5.

2. Two numbers are in ratio 4:7. The sum of numbers is 77. Find numbers.

   4x+7x = 77

   11x = 77

   x = 77/11 = 7

   The numbers are 4 X 7 = 28 and 7 X 7 = 49.

3. Purchase price of 15 articles is 4500. Find number of articles that could be purchased for 1500.

   15:x = 4500 : 1500

   15/x = 4500/1500

   15 X 1500 = 4500x

   15 x 1500/4500 = x

   5 = x.

4. A man covers total distance of 1000 km in 16 hours. Partially by taxi at 36 km/h and partially in a bus at 80 km/h. Distance covered by bus is?

   Taxi : Bus = 36 : 80 or 9 : 20

   Distance = Speed x Time

   Distance covered by taxi = 36 X (16-x)

   Distance covered by Bus = 80 X x

   Total Distance = Distance covered by bus + Distance covered by taxi

   1000 = 80x + 36X16 – 36x

   1000 = 44x + 576

   1000-576 =44x

   424/44 = x

   9.6 = x

   Distance covered by bus = 80 x 9.6 = 768 km

   Distance covered by taxi = 1000-768 = 232 km.

5. Price of TV and Fridge are in the ratio 5:3, if fridge cost Rs. 5500 more than price of tv. Price of fridge is?

   Given that the difference between the price of tv and fridge is 5500.

   Hence, 5x-3x = 2x

   2x = 5500

   x = 5500/2 = 2750

   The price of fridge is 2750 x 5 = Rs. 13750.

Average

Average related to Natural Numbers

I. Average of consecutive natural numbers till n

$$=\frac{(n+1)}{2}$$

II. Average of squares of numbers till n

$$=\frac{(n+1)(2n+1)}{6}$$

III. Average of cubes of consecutive natural numbers till

$$n=\frac{n(n+1)^2}{4}$$

1. Average = Sum of observations / Number of observations
2. Sum of 'n' natural numbers $=\frac{n(n+1)}{2}$
3. Average of 'n' natural numbers $= \frac{\frac{n(n+1)}{2}}{n} = \frac{n(n+1)}{2n} = \frac{(n+1)}{2}$

Questions for practice: -

1. For 9 matches Raman has average of 75 runs. In 10th match he scores 100 runs thus increasing his average. His new average is?

   Solution: Sum = Average x Number

   = 75 x 9 = 675

   New sum = 675 + 100

   New average = 775/10

   = 77.5

2. Average monthly income of P and Q is Rs. 5050. Average monthly income of Q and R is Rs. 6250. And average monthly income of R and P is Rs. 5200. Find monthly income of P.

Solution: Given that:

Average monthly income of P and Q is Rs. 5050, so sum is 5050 x 2 = 10100

Average monthly income of Q and R is Rs. 6250, so sum is 6250 x 2 = 12500

Average monthly income of R and P is Rs. 5200, so sum is 5200 x 2 = 10400

= P+Q+Q+R+R+P = 2P + 2Q + 2R = 10100 + 12500 + 10400

= 2(P + Q + R) = 33000

=P + Q + R = 33000/2

=P + Q + R = 16500

=P + Q + R = 16500

=P = 16500 – 12500

=P = 4000.

1. Average of 9 observations is 9. That of average of first five is 10 and last 5 is 8. What is the fifth observation?

   Solution:

   Sum of total observations= 9 x 9 = 81

   Sum of first five observations = 5 x 10 = 50

   Sum of last five observations = 5 x 8 = 40

   ($1^{st} + 2^{nd} + 3^{rd} + 4^{th} + 5^{th}$) + ($5^{th} + 6^{th} + 7^{th} + 8^{th} + 9^{th}$) = 50 + 40 = 90

$1^{st} + 2^{nd} + 3^{rd} + 4^{th} + 5^{th} + 5^{th} + 6^{th} + 7^{th} + 8^{th} + 9^{th} = 90$

$81 + 5^{th} = 90$

5th observation = 90-81 = 9.

2. Sum of first 60 natural numbers is?

Solution: $= \frac{n(n+1)}{2}$

$= \frac{60(60+1)}{2}$

=30 x 61 = 1830.

3. Average of first 60 natural numbers is?

Solution: Sum/Observations

$= \frac{(n+1)}{2}$

= 61/2 = 30.5

Advanced Mathematical Aptitude

Speed-Distance-Time

1. **Speed, Time and Distance:**

   Speed = $\left(\frac{\text{Distance}}{\text{Time}}\right)$, Time = $\left(\frac{\text{Distance}}{\text{Speed}}\right)$, Distance = (Speed x Time).

2. **km/hr to m/sec conversion:**

   x km/hr = $\left(x \times \frac{5}{18}\right)$ m/sec.

3. **m/sec to km/hr conversion:**

   x m/sec = $\left(x \times \frac{18}{5}\right)$ km/hr.

4. If the ratio of the speeds of A and B is $a : b$, then the ratio of the

   the times taken by then to cover the same distance is $\frac{1}{a} : \frac{1}{b}$ or $b : a$.

5. Suppose a man covers a certain distance at x km/hr and an equal distance at y km/hr. Then,

   the average speed during the whole journey is $\left(\frac{2xy}{x + y}\right)$ km/hr.

Formula:

1. Distance = Speed x Time
2. Speed = Distance/Time
3. Time = Distance/Speed

Questions with Solutions:

1. A person crosses 600 m long street in 5 minutes. Find speed in Kmph.

   Solution: Speed = Distance/Time

   =600/5

   =120 m/min

   =120/1000 x 60

   (1 m = 1/1000 km, 1 min = 1/60 hour. Therefore, 120 m/min = $\frac{120/1000}{1/60}$)

   =7.2 kmph

2. If a person walks at 14 kmph instead of 10 kmph. He could have walked 20 km more than the actual distance travelled by him. Find the actual distance?

Solution:

Let Actual Distance be x

x distance covered in time t with speed of 10 kmph ----Case 1

Time = D/S

t=x/10---------------------------1

x + 20 distance covered in time t with speed of 14 kmph ----Case 2

t = x + 20 / 14-----------------------------2

Equating equation 1 and 2

x/10 = x + 20 / 14

Cross multiplying = x X 14 = 10(x + 20)

14x = 10x + 200

4x = 200

x = 200/4

x = 50 km.

3. A man completes a journey of 61 km in 9 hours. He travels partly on foot at 4 kmph and partly by bicycle at 9 kmph. The distance travelled on foot is?

Solution: $d_1 = x$, $d_2 = 61 - x$, $s_1 = 4$, $s_2 = 9$

$t_1 + t_2 = 9$

d/s + d/s = 9

x/4 + (61 – x) /9 = 9

$= \frac{9x+244-4x}{36} = 9$

9x + 244 – 4x = 9 x 36

5x = 324 – 244

x = 80/5

x= 16 km

Problems on Trains:

Case	Types of Objects	Time to Cross
1.	Object is stationary and is of negligible length e.g. train crosses lamp post, pole, standing man etc.	$t = \frac{\text{Length of Train}}{\text{Speed of Train}}$
2.	Object is stationary and is of some length, e.g. train crosses a bridge, a tunnel, platform, or another train at rest	$t = \frac{\text{Length of (Train+Object)}}{\text{Speed of Train}}$
3.	Object is moving and is of negligible length, e.g. train crosses a running man, a running car etc.	$t = \frac{\text{Length of Train}}{\text{Speed of (Train−Object)}}$
4.	Object is moving and has some length, e.g. train crosses another running train	$t = \frac{\text{Length of (Train+Object)}}{\text{Speed of (Train−Object)}}$

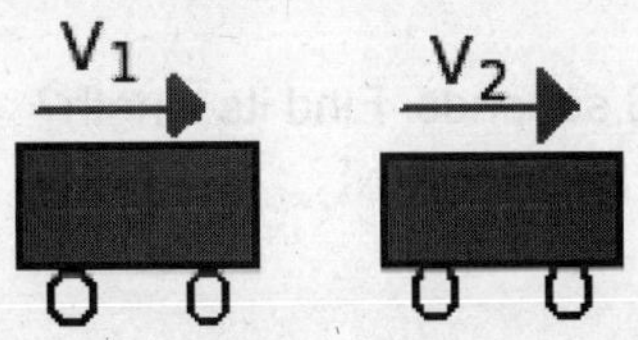

⟶ Relative Speed $= V_1 - V_2$

Objects Moving in Same direction

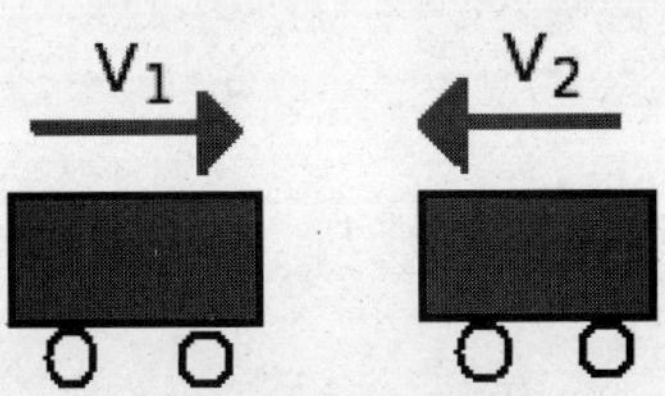

⟶ Relative Speed $= V_1 + V_2$

Objects Moving in Opposite Direction

Formula:

1. Relative Speed (when train moves in opposite direction) = Speed = S1 + S2
2. **Relative Speed (when train moves in same direction) = Speed = S1 - S2 (S1>S2).**
3. **Speed of train =** $\frac{\textbf{\textit{Total distance covered by train}}}{\textbf{\textit{time taken}}}$

Questions with Solutions:

1. If two trains moving towards each other with speed S1= 50 kmph and S2 = 60 kmph. Length of both the trains are 400 m respectively.

   Solution: Time = Distance i.e., length / speed

   T = (L1 + L2)/ S1 + S2

   T = 400 + 400 / 50 + 60

   T = 800 m or 0.8 km / 110

   T = 0.8 / 110

   T = 8 / 1100 hours.

2. If two trains moving with each other with speed S1= 66 kmph and S2 = 60 kmph. Length of both the trains are 400 m respectively.

   Solution: T = (L1 + L2)/ S1 - S2

   T = 400 + 400 / 66 - 60

   T = 800 m or 0.8 km / 6

   T = 0.8 / 6

   T = 8 / 60 or 2/15 hours.

3. A train with the speed of 56 kmph crosses a pole in 18 seconds. Find its length?

   Solution: Speed = Distance / Time

   Speed = 56 x 1000/3600 m/sec.

   = 560/36 = 140/9

   140/9 = Distance i.e., length of train/18

   =140/9 x 18 = Length of train

   =280 meters.

Boat and Streams

1. Speed of Boat in still water: SB
2. Speed of Boat in river/ current/ stream: SS
3. Speed in downstream (with the flow) = SD
4. Speed in Upstream (against the flow) = SU
5. SD = SB + SS
6. SU = SB – SS
7. SB = $\frac{\text{SD + SU}}{2}$
8. SS = $\frac{\text{SD} - \text{SU}}{2}$

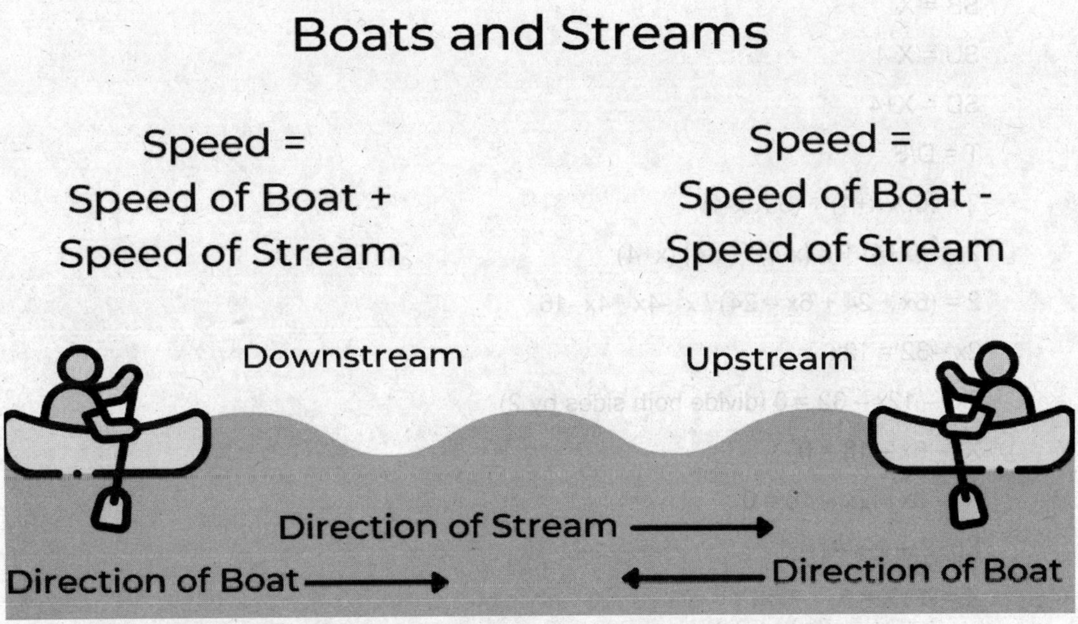

Questions with Solutions:

1. A boat running downstream covers distance of 20 km in 2 hours. While it covers same distance upstream in 5 hours. Find the speed of boat?

   Solution: SD = 10 kmph (d/t=20/2)

   SU = 4 kmph (s=d/t, 20/5 = 4)

   SB = $\frac{\text{SD + SU}}{2}$

   = $\frac{10+4}{2}$ = 14/2 = 7 kmph.

The speed of boat is 7 kmph.

2. Speed of boat along the stream is 12 kmph and against is 8 kmph. Time taken by boat to sail 24 km in still water?

   Solution: SD = 12 kmph, SU = 8 kmph

   $SB = \frac{SD + SU}{2} = \frac{12+8}{2}$ = 20/2 = 10 kmph

   D = 24 km

   T = D/S

   = 24/ 10 = 2.4 hours. Or 2 hours 24 minutes.

3. The current of stream runs at 4 kmph and a boat goes 6 km and comes back to starting point in 2 hours. Find the speed of boat?

   Solution: SS = 4 kmph

   SB = X

   SU = X-4

   SD = X+4

   T = D/S

   2 = (6 X x+4) + (6 X x-4)

   2 = 6(x+4) + 6 (x-4) / (x-4) (x+4)

   2 = (6x + 24 + 6x – 24) / x^2 -4x +4x -16

   $2x^2$ -32 = 12x

   $2x^2$ – 12x – 32 = 0 (divide both sides by 2)

   X^2 – 6x – 16 = 0

   X^2 – 8x + 2x – 16 = 0

   X(x-8)+ 2(x-8) = 0

   X = -2, X = 8

   Hence, speed of boat is 8 kmph.

4. Two boat A and B starts towards each other from two points that are 108 km apart. Speed of boat A is 12 kmph and B is 15 kmph in still water. If A proceeds downstream and B proceeds upstream, they will meet after?

   Solution: D1 = (12 + SS) x T, D2 = (15 - SS) x T

   D1+D2 = (12 + SS) x T + (15 - SS) x T

   D1 + D2 = 12T + SST + 15T – SST

   108 = 12T + 15T

108 = 27T

4 hours = Time taken by boats to meet.

5. Find speed of stream if a boat covers 120 km downstream and 40 km upstream in 4 hours respectively?

Solution: SU = 10 kmph (S = D/T, = 40/4 = 10 kmph)

SD = 30 kmph (S = D/T, = 120/4 = 30 kmph)

$SS = \frac{SD - SU}{2}$

$= \frac{30-10}{2}$

= **10 Kmph is the speed of stream.**

Problem on ages

Statement	Equation
A's age 3 years later (after, hence, down the line)	A+3
A's age 3 years ago	A-3
A is 3 years older than B	A=B+3
A is 3 years younger than B	A=B-3
A is 3 times older than B	A=3B
Father was as old as his son at present, at the time of his birth	F-S = S F=2S
The present age ratio of A and B is 5:6. Four years hence their age ratio will be 6:7	A/B = 5/6 (A+4)/(B+4) = 6:7

Questions with solutions:

1. A is 18 years older to B. Respective ratio of B's age 6 years hence and C's present age is 3:2. If at present A's age is twice the age of C. What is B's age 4 years ago?

Solution: Given- B+6 : C = 3:2 and A = B+18, A=2C

B+6/C = 3/2

2B + 12 = 3C

Putting value of C=A/2

2B + 12 = 3 x A/2

4B + 24 = 3A

Putting value of A as B+18

4B +24 = 3 (B+18)

4B +24 = 3B + 54

B = 30

B's age 4 years ago would be 30 – 4 = 26 years.

2. 5 years ago, Soni's age at that time was 1/3 of Amit's age. The respective ratio between Amit age 6 year hence and Soni's age 12 year hence will be 7:4. Find age of Soni's age 3 years ago?

   Solution: Given: Soni's age (S) – 5 = 1/3(A-5), A+6:S+12 = 7:4

   3S – 15 = A-5

   3S – 10 = A --------------------1

   A+6: S+12 = 7:4

   A+6/S+12 = 7/4

   4A + 24 = 7S+ 84

   4A + 7S = 60

   4(3S-10) + 7S = 60 (from equation 1)

   12S – 40 + 7S = 60

   5S = 100

   S = 20

   Age of Soni 3 year ago would be 20 – 3 = 17.

3. A father said to his son "I was as old as you are at present at time of your birth". If father's age is 38 years now, the son's age 5 years back was?

   Solution: Let present age of son be x

   38-x= x

   38 = 2x

   19 = x

   So, five years back his age would be 19-5 = 14 years.

Profit-Loss and Discount

Cost Price is amount at which shopkeeper buys item

↓

Marked Price is the price is printed on the item

↓

Selling Price is at which item is sold to customer

Marked price – discount = selling price

Marked price $\left(\frac{100-discount}{100}\right)$ = selling price

Cost Price $\frac{(100+profit)}{100}$ = selling price

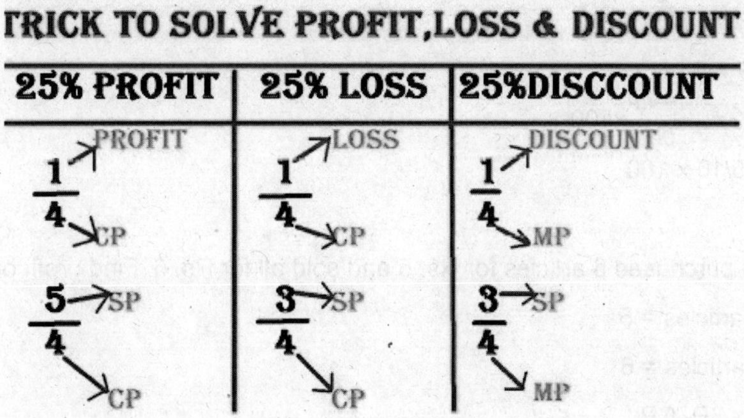

1. CP - Cost Price
2. SP – Selling Price
3. SP = CP + Profit
4. Profit = SP-CP
5. Profit % = $\frac{SP-CP}{CP}$x100

6. Loss = CP-SP
7. Loss % = $\frac{CP-SP}{CP}$x100
8. Profit on CP = P/CP x 100
9. Loss on CP = L/CP x 100
10. SP = Market Price or listed value or listed price – Discount
11. SP + Discount = Market Price
12. Successive Discount: $d_1+d_2 - (\frac{d1\ X\ d2}{100})$

To calculate profit/loss percent, cost price will be base.

1. 20% profit = (20% = 1/5)

   In this, 1 is profit and 5 is cost price.

   To calculate selling price i.e., CP + Profit

   SP = 5+1 =6

   Hence ratio between CP and SP = 5:6
2. 25% Loss = ¼

   Here, 1 is loss and 4 is CP, hence SP = 3

   Ratio between SP and CP is 3:4.
3. CP of 15 article is equal to SP of 10 article. Find profit or loss percentage.

   Solution: 15 CP= 10 SP

   CP/SP = 10/15

   SP-CP = 5

   Profit% =: $\frac{SP-CP}{CP}$x100

   P% = 5/10 x 100

   50%
4. A man purchased 6 articles for Rs. 5 and sold all for Rs. 6. Find profit or loss %?

   CP of articles = 5

   SP of articles = 6

   Profit = SP- CP

   =6-5

   =1

   Profit % =: $\frac{SP-CP}{CP}$x100

   =1/5 x 100

   =**20%**

5. By selling an article for Rs. 240, a man incur loss of 10%. At what price should he sell it to make profit of 20%?

   If he is incurring loss of 10% by selling an article at 240 Rs.

   So 90%=240

   120%=240/90 x 120

   =320.

   If he sells item at Rs.320, he can earn 20% profit.

6. A man sold two articles at 375 each. On one he gains 25% and on other he losses 25%. What is overall gain nor loss?

   Solution: Let profit and loss percent be x

   To calculate over loss or gain the formula is:

   $=x^2/100$

   =-25x25/100

   =-625/100

   =-6.25%

   Hence, overall loss is 6.25%.

7. The profit earned after selling an article for Rs. 1516 is same as loss incurred after selling article for Rs. 1112. Find Cost?

   Solution: Profit = Loss, Let CP be x

   =SP-CP = CP-SP

   1516 – x = x – 1112

   = 2x= 2628

   = x= 1314

   Hence, CP is 1314.

8. An article sold at 16 % profit. If he given Rs. 300 less then there will be loss of 14%. Find CP?

   Solution: 16%+14% = 300

   30% = 300

   100% = 300/30 x 100

   Cost Price = 1000

9. Two successive discounts of 10 % and 20 % are equal to a single discount of?

   Solution:

   = One single discount= $d_1 + d_2 - (\frac{d1 \ X \ d2}{100})$

$= 10+20 - (\frac{10 X 20}{100})$

=30 – 2

=28%.

10. A tradesman marks his goods 20% above the CP. He allows the discount of 8% on MP. Find profit %?

    Solution: Let CP = 100

    MRP would be = 120

    Discount = $\frac{8}{100}$x120 = 9.6

    SP = MP- Discount, 120 -9.6 = 110.4

    P% = SP-CP/CP x100 = 110.4 – 100/100 x 100

    = The profit % is 10.4%.

11. A dishonest shopkeeper promises to sell his article at CP. But he gains 10% profit and he uses 20 % less weight. Find profit %.

    Solution: Let CP be 100

    He is selling 20% less and also gaining 10%.

    For him CP is 80 and SP is 110.

    Profit% = 110-80/80 x 100

    =30/80 x 100

    =37.5 %.

Simple Interest

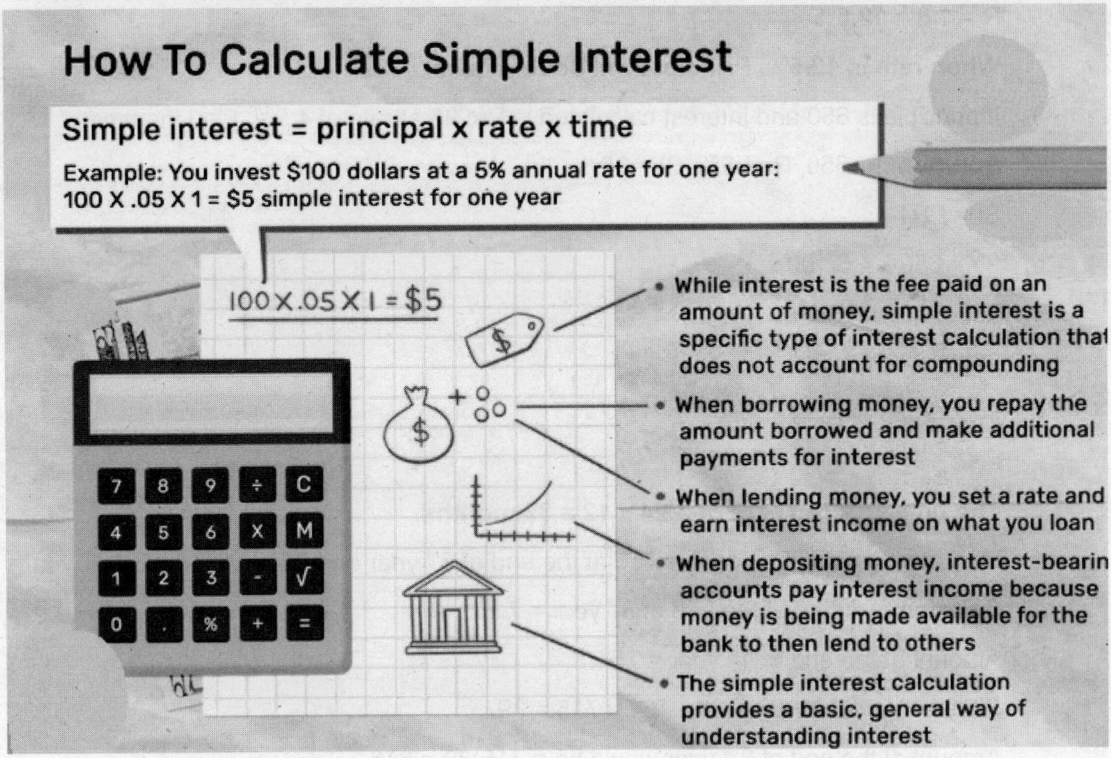

1. Simple Interest = Principle x Rate x Time
2. Amount = Principal + SI
3. In SI, interest and Principal remain constant

Questions with Solutions:

1. Principal = 54000, Rate = 5%, Time = 2 years.

   Solution: SI = PRT

   =54000 x 5/100 x 2

   =540 x 5 x2

   = 5400.

2. What would be the rate of interest if money doubles in 8 years.

   Solution: Let Principal be P, Rate be R, Time = 8 years, SI = P (as P doubles itself), Amount = 2P

   SI = PRT

P = PR8

1 = R8

1/8 = R

R = 1/8 = 12.5%

When rate is 12.5%, Principal will double itself.

3. If principle is 650 and interest calculated is Rs. 95 at rate of 4.5%. Find the time.

   Solution: P=650, R=4.5%, SI = 95.

   SI = PRT

   95 = 650 x 4.5/100 x T

   9500 = 65 x 45 x T

   9500 = 2925 x T

   9500/2925 = T

   = T

   The time is 3.24 Years or 3.24 x 12 = 39 months.

4. Find the principal if amount is 715 at the end of 3rd year and 754 at the end of 4th year.

   Solution: Amount at the end of 3rd year = 715

   Amount at the end of 4th year = 754

   Simple Interest every year = 754 – 715 = 39

   Amount at the end of 2nd year would be = 715-39 = 676

   Amount at the end of 1st year would be = 676 – 39 = 637

   Principle = Amount – SI

   = 637 – 39

   = 598 is the principal.

   OR

   SI for 1 year = 754-715 =39

   SI for 3 years = 39 x 3 = 117

   Principal = Amount – SI

   = 715 – 117

   = 598.

5. A sum of Rs. 1550 was lent partly at 5% and partly at 8%. The interest received after 3 years was Rs. 300. Ratio of money lent at 5% and at 8% is?

   Solution: SI = PRT

Let sum lent at 5% be y and sum lent at 8% be 1550-y.

300 = (y x 5/100 x 3) + (1550-y x 8/100 x 3)

Take 3 and 1/100 common

300 = 3 x 1/100 (y x 5) + (1550-y x 8)

300 x 100/3 = 5y + (1550-y) x 8

10000 = 5y + 12400 – 8y

-2400 = -3y

-2400/-3 = y

800 = y (sum lent at 5% interest)

1550-800 = 750 (sum lent at 8% interest)

Ratio = 800:750

=16:15.

Compound Interest

Compound Interest

Compound interest is calculated on the **principal (original) amount** and on the **interest already accumulated** in previous periods..

$$A = P(1 + \frac{r}{100})^n$$

Where:

A represents the final amount

P represents the original principal amount

r is the interest rate over a given period

n represents the number of times the interest rate is applied over time

Principal	Rate	Time	Interest	Amount
1000	10%	1	100	1100

1100	10%	1+1	110	1210
1210	10%	1+1+1	121	1331

At the end of 3rd year 1000 Rs. becomes 1331.

Facts:

1. CI is always greater than SI.
2. CI and SI are equal in the first year.

Questions with Solutions:

1. Calculate compound interest if principle is 20000 at 10% rate for 3 years.

Solution: CI = P(1+r/100)^t – P

= 20000(1+10/100)^3-20000

=20000(1+.1)^3- 20000

=20000(1.1 x 1.1 x 1.1) – 20000

=20000(1.331) – 20000

=26620 – 20000

=6620.

OR

Principal----R-----T------CI------Amount

20000---10%----1 year-----2000-----22000

22000----10%-----1+1 year------2200------24200

24200------10%-----1+1+1-------2420---------26620

CI at the end of 3rd year = 2000+2200+2420 = **6620.**

2. If CI is 5000 and rate is 5%, find principal amount for 2 years.

Solution: CI = P(1+r/100)^t – P

5000=P (1+5/100)^2-P

5000=P (1.05 x 1.05) – P

5000+P = P (1.1025)

5000/P + 1 = 1.1025

5000/P = 0.1025

5000/0.1025 = P

48780=P.

3. When principal is 15000, rate is 20% and time is half year. Calculate CI.

   Solution: (When CI is to be calculated on half yearly basis, we multiply time with 2 and divide rate with 2.)

   P = 15000, R=20/2, T= ½ x 2

   CI = $P(1+r/100)^{t}$-P

   CI = $15000(1+10/100)^{1}$-15000

   CI = 15000 x 1.1 – 15000

   CI= 16500-15000

   CI = 1500.

Time and Work

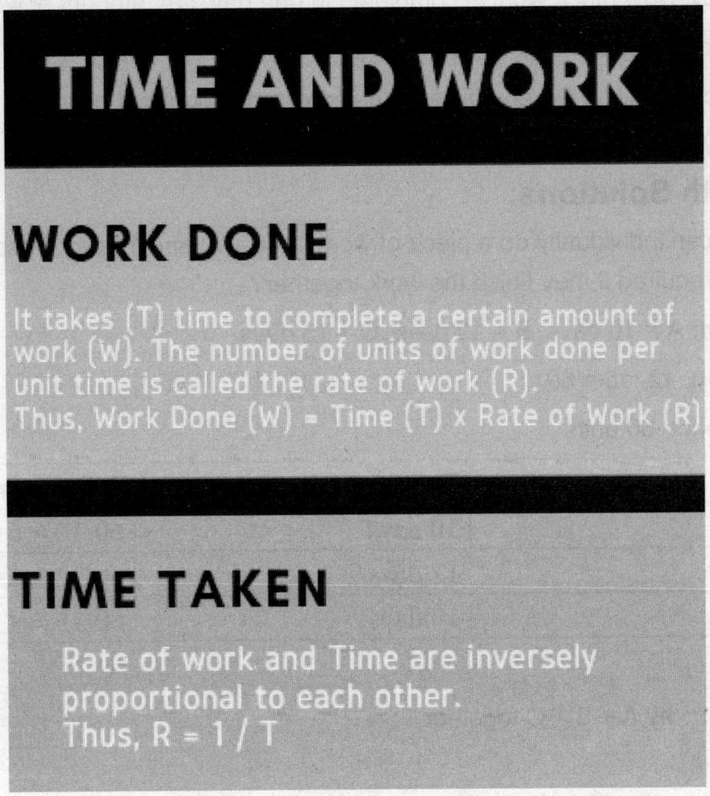

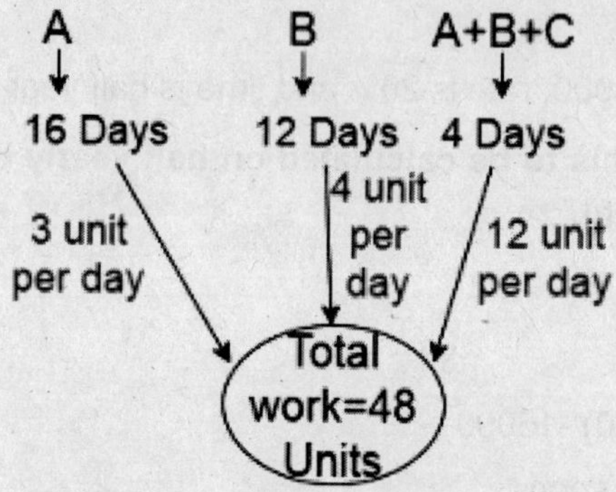

Efficiency of C=eff.(A+B+C) - eff.(A+B)
=12 unit - (3+4)
=5 unit

Concept

1. Determination of work: Building a wall can be determined as one unit/100 unit or anything.
2. Efficiency: How much work is completed in one day, i.e., amount of work in a day.
3. Total Work = Efficiency x Time
4. Efficiency = 1/Time (when efficiency is more, time taken will be less)
5. Time = Work /Efficiency

Questions with Solutions:

1. A, B, C can individually do a piece of work in 10, 12, and 15 days respectively. Number of days required if they finish the work together?

   Solution: A = 10 days, B = 12 days, C = 15 days

   LCM = 10, 12, 15 = 60

   Total work = 60 units

	Days	Efficiency = Work/Time
A	10 days	60/10 = 6 units/day
B	12 days	60/12 = 5 units/day
C	15 days	60/15 = 4 units/day

Work done by A + B + C together

=6 + 5 + 4

=15 units in 1 day

Time in which A, B, C can finish the work = Total work/ Efficiency

=60/15

=4 days.

2. A and B can together do a piece of work in 10 days. A alone can do it in 30 days. Time in which B alone can do is?

Solution: A + B = 10 days

A = 30 days

LCM = 10, 30 = 30

Total work = 30 units

	Days	**Efficiency**
A + B	10 days	30/10 = 3 units/day
A	30 days	30/30 = 1 units/day

Work done by B = (A+B) – A

=3-1

=2

Time in which B can finish the work = Total work/ efficiency of B

=30/2

=15 days.

3. A and B can do a work in 10 days. B and C can do it in 12 days. A and C can do it in 15 days. How long will A take to do it alone?

Solution: LCM = 10, 12, 15 = 60

Total work be 60 units.

	Number of Days	**Efficiency**
A + B	**10**	**60/10 = 6**
B + C	**12**	**60/12 = 5**
C + A	**15**	**60/15 = 4**

A + B + B + A + A + C = (6+5+4)

2A + 2B + 2C = 15

2(A + B + C) = 15

A + B + C = 15/2

A + 5 = 7.5

A = 2.5

Efficiency of A = 2.5 units/day

He alone can complete total work in = Total work/Efficiency

=60/2.5

=600/25

=24 days.

4. A is twice good work man as B and together they finish a piece of work in 14 days. Find the number of days taken by A alone?

Solution: Ratio of Efficiency→ A:B→2:1

Total work = 14 days

A + B complete work in 14 days

Efficiency of A + B = 3

Total work = 3 x 14 = 42

Time taken by A alone= 42/2 = 21 days.

E can complete a job in 6 days, F can do in 9 days, G in 12 days. If E and F started the job and after 3 days G took over and completed it. Find time for which G worked?

Solution: LCM = 6, 9, 12 = 36

Total work = 36

	Days	Efficiency
E	6 days	36/6 = 6 units/day
F	9 days	36/9 = 4 units/day
G	12 days	36/12 = 3 units/day

Work completed in 3 days by E and F = 3 x (6+4) = 30 units.

Remaining work = 36 – 30 = 6 units.

Time taken by G alone = Remaining work/efficiency of G

=6/3

=2

In 2 days, G will complete the remaining work.

5. 12 men and 2 women can complete a work in 5 days, while 3 men and 2 women can do it in 10 days. In how many days will 3 men and 4 women will do?

Solution: (12 M + 2W) x 5 = Total work--------------1

(3M + 2W) x 10 = Total work----------------------------2

From equation 1 and 2

(12M + 2W)5 = (3M + 2W)10

=60M + 10W = 30M + 20W

=30M = 10W

=3M = W--3

(3M + 4W) X days = (3M + 2W)10

W + 4W x days = 30M + 20W

5W x days = 10W + 20W

Days = 30/5

=In 6 Days, 3 men and 4 women will complete the work.

6. A can do a certain amount of work in 10 days while B can do the same work in 20 days. If they work on alternate days, find the number of days taken by them if started by A.

Solution: A → 10 days, B→20 days

LCM (Total work) = 20

Efficiency of A = 20/10 = 2

Efficiency of B = 20/20 = 1

	Days	Work Done/Efficiency
A	10	2 unit/day
B	20	1 unit/day

Day 1→A→2 units

Day 2→B→1 unit

Hence, 3 units in 2 days.

3→x 6 = 18

2→x 6 = 12

In 12 days, 18 units of work was finished. Remaining 2 units will be done by A in 1 day. Therefore, in 13 days 20 units of work will be done.

CHAPTER

6

LOGICAL REASONING

LOGICAL REASONING

DEFINITIONS

A definition of **stipulative** when it assigns a meaning to a word (old or new) for the first time.

A definition is **lexical** when it reports the meaning that a word already has in a language.

A definition is **precising** when it reduces the vagueness of a word.

A definition is **theoretical** when the meaning of a word is suggested by a theory which assigns a characterization to the word.

A definition is **persuasive** when it influences to a favorable or unfavorable attitude towards the word that is defined.

Deductive argument: General to Particular.

If the premises are true, the conclusion is always true.

P1: All dogs have long ears

P2: Tommy is a dog

C: Tommy has long ears.

Inductive Argument: Particular to general

If the premises are true, the conclusion not always be true.

P1: Tommy has long ears.

P2: Tommy is a dog

C: All dogs have long ears

Valid arguments: if the conclusion follows premises, then the argument is valid. I.e.

If the premises are true, the conclusion is also true.

If one premise is true, the conclusion may be true or false.

Square of Opposition

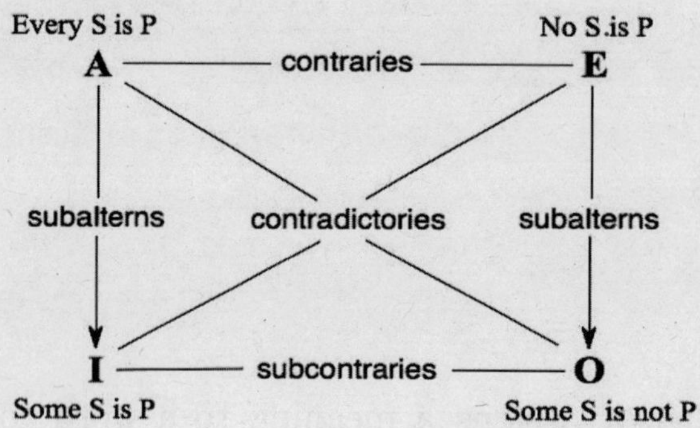

A propositions or universal affirmatives take the form: All S are P.

E propositions, or universal negations take the form: No S are P.

I proposition, or particular affirmatives take the form: Some S are P.

O propositions or particular negations take the form: Some S are not P

Propositions are contradictory when the truth of one implies the falsity of the other, and conversely. Both cannot be true or false at the same time.

Propositions are contrary when they cannot both be true; if one is true, then the other must be false. They can both be false. A and E propositions are contrary.

Propositions are subcontrary when it is impossible for both to be false; if one is false then the other must be true. They can both be true.

Two propositions are said to stand in the relation of Subalternation when the truth of the first ("the superaltern") implies the truth of the second ("the subaltern"), but not conversely.

- If universal Is true, particular will be true definitely.
- If universal is false, particular will be doubtful,
- If particular is false, universal will be false definitely.
- If particular is true, universal will be doubtful.

Formal Fallacies

- Most formal fallacies are errors of logic, where the Conclusion is not supported by the premises,
- Premise: All black bugs are carnivores.
- Premise: All rats are carnivores.
- Conclusion: All rats are black bugs.

Informal Fallacies

Informal fallacies take many forms. They are widespread in our routine lives. (error in content). Informal fallacies develop when

- The relationship between premises and conclusion does not hold up.
- When premises are unsound.
- Informal fallacies are more dependent on the misuse of language and evidence.

1. Accidental fallacy

The fallacy occurs when one attempts to apply a general rule to an irrelevant situation.

For example:

- Cutting people with knives is a crime.
- Surgeons cut people with knives.
- Surgeons are criminals

2. Ad populum (Bandwagon)

Also referred to as the bandwagon fallacy, the arguer tries to convince the audience to do or believe something because everyone else (supposedly) does

Example:

- An increasing number of people are turning to yoga as a way to get in touch with their inner-being
- Therefore, yoga helps one get in touch with their inner being

3. Red Herring

Attempts to distract from the main issue by bringing in irrelevant information.

For example, an argument against raising salaries might go something like this: "We can't raise salaries, but we still provide great benefits for our employees." This argument is a red herring because the mention of employee benefits distracts from the real point, that salaries will not be raised.

4. The complex question fallacy

The complex question fallacy is committed when someone asks a question that presupposes something that has not been proven or accepted by everyone involved.

Example: " Have you stopped cheating on exams?

5. Fallacy of Division

Assuming that what is true of the whole is true for the parts.

Example: That car is blue. Therefore, its engine is blue.

Example: Your family is weird. That means that you are weird too.

6. Appeal to ignorance

This logical fallacy occurs when someone claims that a conclusion must be true if it hasn't been proven false, or false if it hasn't been proven true.

Example:

"You can't prove that you are innocent, therefore you are guilty to me."

7. Hasty Generalization

This logical fallacy occurs when someone draws a conclusion based on just a small sample size. In other words, the conclusion is supported by insufficient evidence.

Example

"My friend has been eating only hamburgers, pizza, and fries for 10 years, and he has no health issues. Therefore, fast food is not unhealthy for you.

8. Slippery Slope

Assuming that one relatively insignificant event will have a series of unintended consequences and lead to some significant outcome.

Example

"If we legalize marijuana now, next they will legalize all the other drugs, and then crime will explode."

9. Ad Hominem (Abusive)

Attacking the person making the argument, rather than the argument itself, when the attack on the person is completely irrelevant to the argument the person is making.

Example: Suppose it's your partner's responsibility to take the garbage out. You remind them. They say they'll do it later because it's raining. You say it's not raining and they say, "You just like bossing me around." That's an attack on your motives for saying it's not raining.

Moods and figures:

Categorical Syllogism:

1. All good logicians are beer lovers – P1
2. No politicians are good logicians – P2
3. Some politicians are not beer lovers – C

   Subject (Minor term) – Politicians

   Predicate (major term) – beer lovers

The middle term is not in the conclusion but in both premises i.e. Good logicians

A – All　　P1 – A

E – Not　　P2 – E

I – Some　　C – O　　Mood = A E O

Figures -	Fig 1	Fig 2	Fig 3	Fig 4
	Midterm L to R	R in both	L in both	Midterm R to L

The figure of the above syllogism is 1

Venn Diagram Questions

Given below are two premises and four conclusions are drawn from them staking beingly or together). Select the code that states the conclusions validly drawn.

Premises:

(i) All religious persons are emotional

(ii) Ram is a religious person.

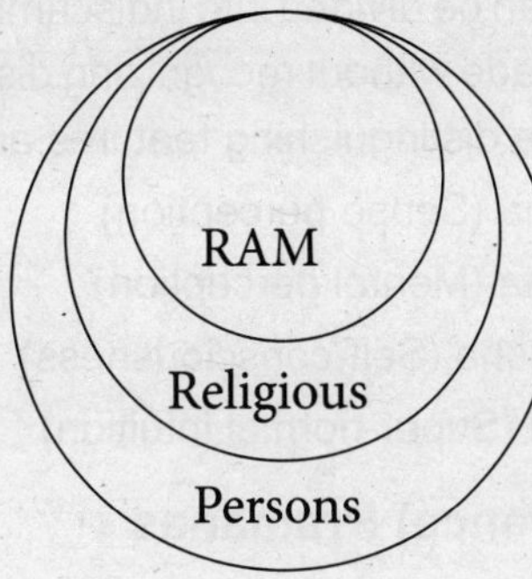

Conclusions:

(a) Ram is emotional.

(b) All emotional persons are religious.

(c) Ram is not a non-religious person

(d) Some religious persons are not

Emotional.

Codes

1. (a), (b), (c), and (d)
2. (a) only
3. (a) and (c) only
4. (b) and (c) only

Answer – 3

Indian Logic: Means of knowledge

Pramanas: 'Proof', 'Means of knowledge' study of the science of Pramanas is called 'न्याय'

Six Pramas:

1. Pratyaksha Perception [straightforward]
2. Anumana Inference [Guess]
3. Upamana Comparison [Analogy]
4. Arthapatti [implication] Derivation from circumstances [Assume]
5. Anuplabdhi Non-perception [no proof]
6. Sabda Word, testimony

➢ Pratyaksa (Perception)

The word 'pratyaksa' consists of two parts viz. "prati" meaning near or before or related to and "aksi" meaning eye. So, it means the process through which immediate knowledge of an object arises or it means the instrument by which the object is conceived.

Types of Pratyaksha

Pratyaksha is broadly divided into two types:

- **Direct perception (Anubhava):** In this type of perception, the knowledge of an object arises when it comes in contact with sense organs; smell (nose), touch (skin), form (eyes), sound (ears), and taste (tongue).
- **Remembered perception (smriti):** The knowledge of an object is based on memory (smriti). Once we have seen a table, it is memorised and when the table again appears in front of us, we can easily be recognized it, what is this?
- Alternatively, It can be divided into indiscriminate perception (nirvikalpa) where the perception of the object is made without recognizing distinguishing features, and discriminate perception (savikalpa) where distinguishing features are observed.
- Indriya pratyaksha (Sense perception)
- Manas pratyaksha (Mental perception)
- Svadana pratyaksha (Self-consciousness)
- Yoga pratyaksha (Super-normal intuition)

➢ Anumana (inference) Pramanas

Anumana means such knowledge that follows some other knowledge. Anumana (inference) is the knowledge of an object due to previous knowledge of some sign or mark. In Anumana Pramana, we arrive at the knowledge of an object through the medium of two acts of knowledge or propositions.

1. Perceptual evidence: We see smoke on the hill
2. Invariable concomitance: Wherever there is smoke, there is fire, as seen in the kitchen.
3. Conclusion: Therefore the hill has a fire

➢ Sabda (word, testimony) Pramanas

A universal way of communication is either an oral or written message, and we learn mostly through words. We continuously get various information, direction, and knowledge through words. Since school days, we use words as a valid and effective means of bringing about awareness of things, ideas, or emotions. Books, magazines, newspapers, letters, conversations, chats, radio, TV, movies, songs, etc., all depend on words.

➢ Upamana (Comparison, analogy) Pramanas

- Upamana is the process by which the knowledge of B's similarity to C is gained from the perception of C's similarity to B, which has been seen elsewhere.
- For example, a person who has seen his cow in a town goes to a forest and sees a wild cow (gavaya). The person sees the similarity "This wild cow is like my cow", and on this basis, he also concludes the opposite to be equally true, that "My cow is like this wild cow.

➢ Arthapatti (postulation, presumption) Pramanas

- Arthapatti is a method of assumption of an unknown fact to account for a known fact that is otherwise difficult. Arthapatti can either be from what is seen or from what is heard.
- One of the classic examples of this method of knowledge is Shyam; a fat person says that he never eats during the day time, then we can easily postulate that he eats at night.

➢ **Anupalabdhi**

- Anupalabdhi means non-apprehension. Its non-perception apprehends the non-existence of a thing.
- There is no teacher in the classroom. There is no sound here. "

➢ **Points to remember:**

- Pratinjna: hypothesis
- Hetu: reason (middle term)
- Nigamana: conclusion
- Vyapti: invariable concomitance between hetu(middle term) and sadhya (major term)

FALLACIES OF INFERENCE

In Indian logic, a fallacy is known as hetvâbhâsa. This fallacy means, the middle term appears to be a reason but is not a valid reason.

1) Savyabhichâra,2) Viruddha, 3) Satpratipaka, 4) Asiddha, and 5)Bâdhita.

1. Savyabhichâra or the fallacy of irregular middle: A middle term may be irregularly related to the major term. When the middle is not uniformly related to the major term then that is called savyabhicâra hetu.

- Let us take the following example,
- All bipeds are rational.
- Swans are bipeds.
- Therefore, swans are rational.

Here, the middle term is 'biped'. But it is not uniformly related to the major term 'rational'. The middle term in this example may be related to both rational and non-rational creatures. Therefore, it is a defective hetu.

2) Viruddha or the contradictory middle: The viruddha hetu or the contradictory middle is that hetu, which though offered to establish the existence of the sâdhya actually establishes the non-existence of the sâdhya; e.g. 'sound is eternal because it is produced'- here, the middle term 'produced' does not prove the eternality of sound, but proves its non-eternality. Here, the middle term itself disproves the original proposition and proves its contradictory.

3) Satpratipaka or the inferentially contradicted middle: When a hetu that is advanced to establish a particular sâdhya in inference is validly contradicted by another hetu which proves the non-existence of the sâdhya of the first inference, the fallacy of satpratipaka arises.

In this case, the first hetu is called satpratipaka hetu.

For example, 'sound is eternal because it is audible' is validly contradicted by another inference 'sound is non-eternal because it is produced like a pot.' Here, the middle term of the first inference, 'audible' is contradicted by the middle term of the second inference 'produced.'

4) Asiddha or the unproved middle: The asiddha hetu is one which is not yet proved, but requires to be proved, like the sâdhya. This means that the asiddha hetu is not a proved or a fact, but an asiddha or unproved assumption.

Let us take an example, 'sky lotus is fragrant because it has lotuses in it like a natural lotus. The middle term of the argument is yet to be proved because we are yet to establish the existence of sky lotus.

5)Bâdhita hetu or the non-inferentially contradicted middle: The middle term of inference may be contradicted by some other 'stronger'means of knowing, such as perception, testimony, etc.

It cannot prove the major term which is disproved by another stronger source of valid knowledge, e.g., 'fire is cold because it is a substance'. Here the middle term 'substance' becomes contradicted because its major term 'coldness' is directly contradicted by perception.

These are the five kinds of defective hetus recognized in Indian logic.

CHAPTER 7

DATA INTERPRETATION

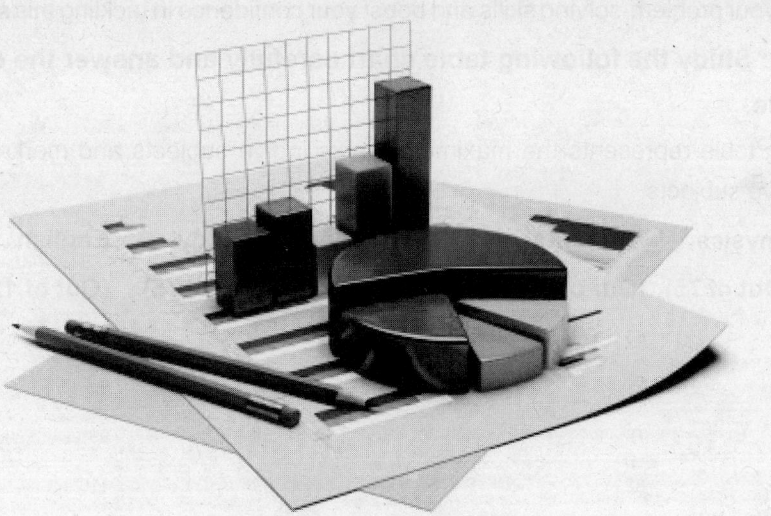

Data Interpretation

Data interpretation involves analyzing and understanding the information presented in various forms, such as graphs, charts, and tables, in order to answer questions based on that information. It is important to have a strong grasp of other numerical ability topics to effectively solve the subparts within each data interpretation question.

Here are some important tips and tricks to solve data interpretation questions effectively:

1. **Improve your calculations:** Data interpretation questions often involve mathematical calculations. Practice regularly to improve your calculation speed and accuracy. Solve different model questions to enhance your calculation skills.
2. **Analyze the question properly:** Carefully analyze the given question and the data provided. Practice solving questions of varying difficulty levels to familiarize yourself with different types of data interpretation questions and improve your speed in solving them.
3. **Focus on speed and accuracy:** Data interpretation requires comfort with numbers,

calculations, fractions, and percentages. Develop shortcut tricks for cube, square, multiplication, and other commonly used calculations. Practice different approaches to solving questions to enhance your accuracy and speed.

4. **Avoid using a calculator:** Since calculators are not allowed in exams, practice solving questions without relying on a calculator. This will help you become more proficient in mental calculations and improve your problem-solving skills.
5. **Pay attention to units:** When solving data interpretation questions, be mindful of units. Many candidates make the mistake of neglecting units, leading to incorrect answers. Practice writing the units along with the answers to reinforce their importance.

Remember, consistent practice and familiarity with different types of data interpretation questions will enhance your problem-solving skills and boost your confidence in tackling this section effectively.

1. Direction: Study the following table chart carefully and answer the questions given beside.

The following table represents the maximum marks in five subjects and marks obtained by five students in five subjects.

Students	Physics (Out of 75)	Mathematics (Out of 100)	Chemistry (Out of 75)	Biology (Out of 75)	English (Out of 120)
Neha	65	65	54	38	95
Nancy	60	52	62	46	99
Nakul	50	78	70	58	99
Nikita	58	82	56	69	110
Naman	42	96	64	72	104

1.1. Marks obtained by Neha in Chemistry and Biology together is what percent of the marks obtained by Nikita in Physics and Mathematics together?

Solution: Marks obtained by Neha in Chemistry and Biology = 54+38 = 92

Marks obtained by Nikita in physics and mathematics = 82+58 = 140

92 is what percent of 140

141 x percent/100 = 92

Percent = 9200/140

= 65.71%

1.2. Find the respective ratio of the marks obtained by all the students in Mathematics and marks obtained by all the students in Chemistry.

Solution: Marks obtained by the students in mathematics: 65+52+78+82+96 = 373

Marks obtained by students in chemistry: 54+62+70+56+64 = 306

Therefore, the ratio is 373:306.

1. 3. Find the overall percentage of Nakul in all the subjects.

Solution: Marks obtained by Nakul in all the subjects: 50+78+70+58+99 =355

Total marks: 445(75+75+100+75+120)

Percentage = Obtained/Total x 100

=355/445 x 100

= 79.77%

1. 4. Find the difference between the percentage of marks obtained by Naman in English and that of Nancy in Physics.

Solution: Marks obtained by Naman in English = 104 out of 120

The percent is 104/120 x 100 = 86.66%

Marks obtained by Nancy in physics: 60 out of 75

The percent is 60/75 x 100 = 80%

The difference between the percentage of marks of Naman and Nancy is 86.66 - 80 = 6.66%.

1.5. Find the change in the percentage of marks obtained by Nancy in all the subjects if her marks got changed in English by 89 instead of 99.

Solution: Marks obtained by Nancy in all the subjects =60+52+62+46+99 = 319

Percentage = 319/445 x 100 =71.6%

If her marks get reduced by 10 (99-89=10), her percentage would be = 309/445 x 100 = 69.43%.

The change **in percent is 71.6 – 69.43 = 2.17%.**

2. Directions: Study the following table chart carefully and answer the questions given below.
The table shows the classification of 80 students based on the marks obtained by them in three different subjects i.e., maths, physics and chemistry.

Maximum marks = 100, Total students = 80

Marks → Subjects→	80 and above marks	60 and above marks	40 and above marks	20 and above marks	0 and above marks
Maths	5	12	70	75	80
Physics	2	18	40	75	80
Chemistry	9	13	35	60	80

2.1. How many students get 40 marks and above but less than 80 marks in all individual subjects?

Solution: Students getting 40 and above marks = 70 + 40 + 35 = 145

Students getting 80 and above marks = 5 + 2 + 9 = 16

Students getting 40 and above marks but less than 80 marks = 145 – 16 = 129

2.2. What Number of students who got 40 marks and above in Chemistry is what percentage of the number of students who got less than 60 marks in Maths?

Solution: Students getting 40 marks and above in Chemistry = 35

Students who get 60 marks and above in Maths = 12

Students who get less than 60 marks in Maths = 80 – 12 = 68

$$\text{Reqd. \%} = \frac{35 \times 100}{68} = 51.47\%$$

2.3. If the passing mark in each subject is 40, then find the percentage of students who passed in Chemistry.

Solution: Students getting 40 marks and above in Chemistry = 35

$$\text{Reqd. \%} = \frac{35 \times 100}{80} = 43.75\%$$

2.4. Find the ratio of the number of students who got less than 20 marks in Maths to the number of students who got less than 40 marks in Chemistry?

Solution: Students getting 20 and above in Maths = 75

Students getting less than 20 = 80 – 75 = 5

Students getting 40 and above in Chemistry = 35

Students getting less than 40 = 80 – 35 = 45

Required ratio = 5: 45 = 1 : 9

2.5. Find the average number of students who got less than 60 marks in Maths, Physics, and Chemistry together?

Solution: Students getting 60 marks and above in Maths = 12

Students getting less than 60 marks in Maths = 80 – 12 = 68

Students getting 60 marks and above in Physics = 18

Students getting less than 60 marks in Physics = 80 – 18 = 62

Students getting 60 marks and above in Chemistry = 13

Students getting less than 60 marks in Chemistry = 80 – 13 = 67

$$\text{Reqd. average} = \frac{68+62+67}{3} = 65.6$$

3. Directions: Study the following table chart carefully and answer the questions given beside.

The following table shows the number of different items in different shops and their respective Selling Price.

Shops	Total No. of Items	AC : Cooler : Fan	Selling Price		
			AC	Cooler	Fan
A	5000	4 : 5 : 1	8000	25000	8500
B	1800	3 : 2 : 4	10000	20000	16000
C	3400	6 : 4 : 7	6000	42000	15000
D	3600	4 : 2 : 3	12000	32000	8000
E	4000	5 : 1 : 4	8000	26500	12200
F	1210	2 : 4 : 5	11000	28000	11100

Solution:

Shops	Total No. of Items	AC : Cooler : Fan	No. of AC	No. of cooler	No. of Fan	Selling Price		
						AC	Cooler	Fan
A	5000	4 : 5 : 1	5000x4/10 = 2000	2500	500	8000	25000	8500
B	1800	3 : 2 : 4	1800x3/9 = 600	400	800	10000	20000	16000
C	3400	6 : 4 : 7	3400x6/17 = 1200	800	1400	6000	42000	15000
D	3600	4 : 2 : 3	3600x4/9 = 1600	800	1200	12000	32000	8000
E	4000	5 : 1 : 4	4000x5/10 = 2000	400	1600	8000	26500	12200
F	1210	2 : 4 : 5	1210x2/11 = 220	440	550	11000	28000	11100
Sum	19010		7620	5340	6050	55000	1,73,500	70800

3.1. Find the number of coolers in all the shops together.

Solution: The number of coolers in all the shops altogether is: 5340

3.2 .Find the percentage of total income which comes from Cooler from shop D.

Solution: Number of coolers sold by shop D = 800

The selling price of the cooler = 32000

Total income of shop D = Selling price of AC x number of AC + Selling price of cooler x number of cooler + Selling price of fan x number of fan

= 12000 x 1600 + 32000 x 800 + 8000 x 1200

= 1,92,00,000 + 2,56,00,000 + 96,00,000

=5,44,00,000

% of income from cooler = 2, 56,00,000/5,44,00,000 x 100

=256/544 x 100

=47.05%

3.3. Find the total income earned by shop B?

Solution: Total income of shop B = Selling price of AC x number of AC + Selling price of cooler x number of the cooler + Selling price of fan x number of fan

=600x10000 + 400x20000 + 800x16000

=60,00,000 + 80,00,000 + 1,28,00,000

=2,68,00,000.

3.4. How much percent of Income in Shop F is from AC?

Solution: Income from Ac in shop F = 220 x 11000 = 24,20,000

Total income of shop F = 440 x 28000 + 11100 x 550 + 24,20,000

=1,23,20,000 + 61,05,000 + 24,20,000

=2,08,45,000

% of income from Ac = 2420000/20845000 x 100

=11.60%.

3.5. What is the ratio between the earnings by the sale of Fan in shop B and shop F?

Solution: Earnings by sale of Fan in shop B = 800 x 16000 = 1,28,00,000

Earnings by sale of Fan in shop F = 550 x 11100 = 61,05,000

Ratio = 12800:6105

=2560:1221.

4. Study the given data to answer the questions given below:

Year	Rice	(Consumption) Wheat	(Grams per day) Coarse Grains	Pulses
1960-62	161	62	131	66
1970-72	197	81	117	64
1980-82	187	116	103	46
1990-92	189	124	102	44
2000-02	201	137	86	64

4.1. For which set of years of the combined consumption per day is equal to other set of years?

Year	Rice	(Consumption) Wheat	(Grams per day) Coarse Grains	Pulses	Sum
1960-62	161	62	131	66	420
1970-72	197	81	117	64	459
1980-82	187	116	103	46	452
1990-92	189	124	102	44	459
2000-02	201	137	86	64	488

The combined consumption is the same for 1970-72 and 1990-92.

4.2. What is the percentage of the average consumption of wheat for the given set of years to the average consumption of total grains? (approx)

Sum of Consumption of wheat in all the years = 62+81+116+124+137 = 520

Average = Sum/number

=520/5

=104

Sum of all grains = 420+459+452+459+488 = 2278

Average = 2278/5

=455.6

Average of wheat is what % of average of all grains

=104 is x % of 455.6

=104 = 455.6 * x/100

=104/456 = x/100

=.2280 x 100 = x

=22.80 = x

Hence, 22.80 grams is a percent of the average consumption of wheat for the given set of years to the average consumption of total grains.

4.3 .For which food grain consumption, was there successive decrease over the given set of years?

Solution: **We just need to observe the table and find in which grain there is continuous fall. As we can see in coarse grains, there is successive decrease over the given set of years.**

4.4. For coarse grains, for the given set of years, the lowest consumption is approximately what percent of that of all grain's consumption per day in such a set of years?

Solution: The lowest consumption of coarse grains is 86 in year 2000-02.

The total of all grains in 2000-02 is 488.

86 is what % of 488

=86/488 x 100 = x

17.62%.

4.5. How much more percentage of the average consumption of Rice than the average consumption of Coarse grains?

Solution: Average consumption of rice = 161+197+187+189+201 = 935

=935/5 = 187

Average consumption of coarse grains = 131+117+103+102+86 = 539

= 539/5 = 107.8

Increase in % = 187-107.8/107.8 x 100

=80.8/107.8 x 100

=.74953 x 100

=74.95%.

CHAPTER 8

INFORMATION AND COMMUNICATION TECHNOLOGY

Information and Communication Technology (ICT)

- ICT: meaning, advantages, disadvantages, and uses
- General abbreviations and terminology
- Basics of Internet and e-mailing
- Transmission modes

There are three primary types of transmission modes based on the direction of exchange of information.

- The first is simplex, followed by half duplex, and finally full duplex.
- Examples of simplex mode are Keyboard and monitor.
- Example of a half-duplex mode is Walkie-Talkies.
- Example of full-duplex mode is Telephone.

Simplex Mode	Half-duplex Mode	Full-duplex Mode
The communication is unidirectional.	The communication is bidirectional, but one at a time.	The communication is bidirectional.
A device can only data but cannot receive it or it can only receive data but cannot send it.	Both the devices can send and receive the data, but one at a time	Both the devices can send and receive the data simultaneously
The lowest performance among the mods.	The performance is better than simplex but less than full duplex	The highest performance among the mods
Examples are radio, keyboard, and monitor	Example is Walkie-Talkies	Example is a telephone or mobile network

Hardware	Software
Hardware is further divided into four main categories: • Input Devices • Output Devices • Secondary Storage Devices • Internal Components	Software is further divided into two main categories: • Application Software • System Software
Developed using electronic and other materials	Developed writing using instructions using a programming language
When damaged, it can be replaced with a new component	When damaged it can be installed once more using a backup copy
Hardware is physical in nature and hence one can touch and see hardware	The software cannot be physically touched but still can be used and seen
Hardware cannot be infected by Viruses	The software can be infected by Viruses
An example of Hardware is hard drives, monitors, CPU, scanners, printers etc.	An example of software is Windows 10, Adobe Photoshop, Google Chrome etc.

TYPES OF HARDWARE

➢ INTERNAL HARDWARE

Internal hardware is also called components. It includes

- CPU
- Motherboard
- RAM
- ROM

Central Proccessing Unit (CPU)

It is the brains of the computer.

Most of the calculations take place here.

Two typical components of a CPU are

- Arithmetic Logic Unit (ALU)
- Control Unit (CU)

Motherboard

- Is the main circuit board of a microcomputer.
- It contains the CPU, memory, expansion slots, and all the controllers required to control standard hardware devices.

Random Access Memory (RAM)

- RAM is the place in a computer where the operating system, application programs, and data in current use are kept.
- It is a temporary memory and can be compared to a person's short-term memory

Read-Only Memory (ROM)

It is a technology that allows you to write data only once. After the data has been written, you can read it an unlimited number of times.

RAM

➢ INPUT HARDWARE

Input hardware consists of external devices by which we give information and instructions to the computer.

Common input hardware are:

- Keyboard
- Mouse
- Scanner

Keyboard

The set of typewriter-like keys that enables you to enter data into a computer

Mouse

A device that controls the movement of the cursor or pointer on a display screen

Scanner

A device that can read text or illustrations printed on paper and translate the information into a form the computer can use.

Scanner

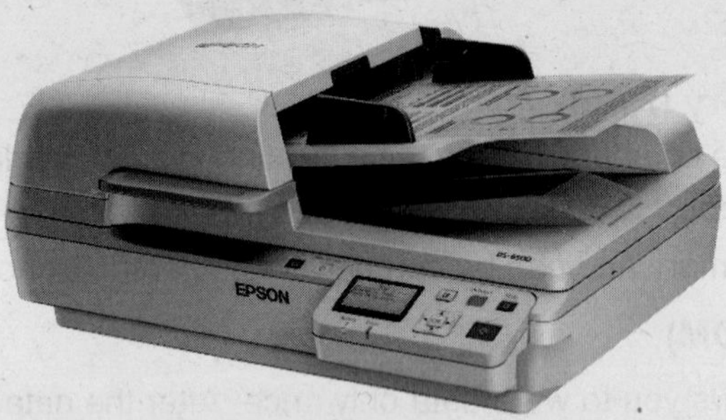

➢ OUTPUT HARDWARE

Output hardware consists of internal and external devices that transfer information from the computer's CPU to the computer user.

Common output hardware are:

- Monitor
- Printer
- Speaker

Monitor

A display screen is used to present output from a computer, video camera, VCR, or other video generator.

Printer

In computers, a printer is a device that accepts text and graphic output from a computer and transfers the information to paper

Speaker

Speakers or headphones to an output port to hear the audio produced by the computer.

➢ CONNECTING HARDWARE

Connecting device allow hardware devices to communicate with each other Common devices are

- Modem
- LAN Card

Modem

Modems connect a personal or portable computer to dial-up networks through a regular telephone line

Lan Card

A Local Area Network (LAN) card is used to provide wireless Internet access to computer users in home or roaming networks.

➢ STORAGE HARDWARE

A computer storage device is any type of hardware that stores data. Some common storage devices are

- Hard Disc
- Floppy Disc
- CD ROM

Hard Disc

A magnetic disk on which you can store computer data. The term hard is used to distinguish it from a soft, or Floppy disk.

Floppy Disc

A flexible plastic disk coated with magnetic material and covered by a protective jacket, used primarily by computers to store data magnetically.

Cd Rom

A CD-ROM is a CD that can be read by a computer with an optical drive

SOFTWARE

- A set of instructions that enables physical components of a computer to work in a synchronized way is known as Software.
- This set of instructions is often called a program.
- Computers cannot do any useful work without instructions from software

➢ TYPES OF SOFTWARE

Computer software is also divided in four major types

- System Software
- Application Software
- Utility Software
- Programming Software

System Software

System software helps in running the computer hardware and the computer system.

Main system soft wares are

- Operating systems
- Device drivers

Operating Systems

An operating system is an interface between hardware and user; it is responsible for the management and coordination of activities and the sharing of the limited resources of the computer.

Device Drivers

In computing, a device driver is a computer program allowing higher-level computer programs to interact with a hardware device

Application Software

It enables the users to accomplish certain specific tasks. Following are the types of application software

Web Browsing Software

It allows one to surf the Web. Example MS Internet Explorer

Word Processing Software

Allows users to create, and edit a document. Example MS Word

Spreadsheet Software

Allows users to create documents and perform calculations. Example: MS Excel etc.

Database Software

Allows users to store and retrieve vast amounts of data. Example: MS Access etc.

Presentation Graphics Software

Allows users to create a visual presentation. Example MS PowerPoint

Utility Software

Utility software helps in the management of computer hardware and application software. It performs a small range of tasks.

Some typical examples of utility software are

Backup

This utility makes a copy of all information stored on a disk, and restore either the entire disk or selected files

Anti-Virus

These utilities scan computer for viruses.

Programming Software

- This is one of the most commonly known and popularly used forms of computer software. This software come in the form of tools that assist a programmer in writing computer Programs.
- The tools that help the programmers in instructing a computer system include

  a. text editors

  a. compilers

  a. interpreters

A compiler is a software that converts the source code to the object code. In other words, we can say that it converts the high-level language to machine/binary language.

Compiler	Interpreter
• A compiler takes the entire program in one go.	• An interpreter takes a single line of code at a time.
• The compiler generates an intermediate machine code.	• The interpreter never produces any intermediate machine code.
• The compiler is best suited for the production environment.	• An interpreter is best suited for a software development environment.
• The compiler is used by programming languages such as C, C ++, C #, Scala, Java, etc.	• An interpreter is used by programming languages such as Python, PHP, Perl, Ruby, etc.

Memory

- Primary memory is the computer's main memory and stores data temporarily.
- Secondary memory is external memory and saves data permanently.
- Data stored in primary memory can be directly accessed by the CPU, which cannot be accessed in secondary memory.

Primary storage	Secondary storage
Data is processed directly from storage.	Data must be moved to primary storage.
Provides faster access time.	Slow access time
Has slower storage capacity.	Has higher storage capacity.
Found inside the Central Processing Unit.	Found outside the Central Processing Unit.

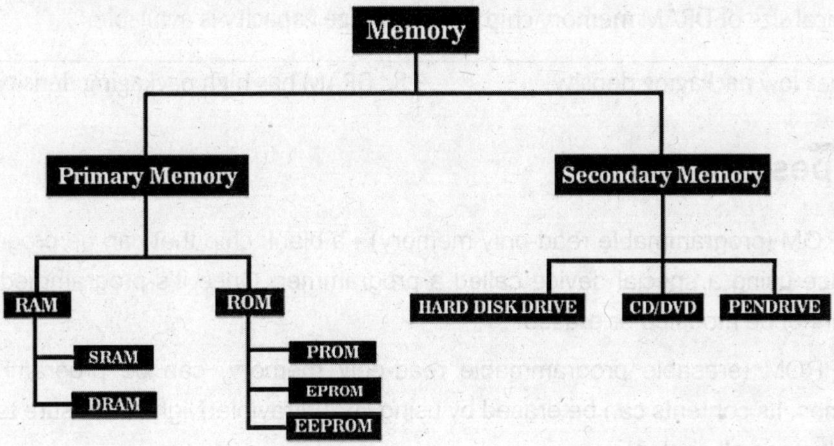

RAM	ROM
1. Temporary Storage.	1. Permanent storage.
2. Store data in MBs.	2. Store data in GBs.
3. Volatile.	3. Non-volatile.
4.Used in normal operations.	4. Used for startup process of computer.
5. Writing data is faster.	5. Writing data is slower.

Difference between RAM and ROM

SRAM	DRAM
1. SRAM has lower access tlme, so lt is faster compared to DRAM.	1. DRAM has higher access tlme, so lt is slower than SRAM.
2. SRAM is costlier than DRAM.	2. DRAM costs less compared to SRAM.
3. SRAM requires constant power supply, whlch means this type of memory consumes more power.	3. DRAM offers reduced power consumption, due to the fact that the information is stored in the capacitor.
4. Due to complex internal circuitry, less storage capaclty is avallable compared to the same physical size of DRAM memory chip.	4. Due to the small internal clrcultry in the one-blt memory cell of DRAM, the large storage capacity is available.
5. SRAM has low packaging density.	5. DRAM has high packaging density.

Other types of ROM

1. PROM (programmable read-only memory) - a blank chip that can be programmed only once using a special device called a programmer. Once it's programmed its contents cannot be modified or erased.
2. EPROM (erasable programmable read-only memory) can be programmed multiple times. Its contents can be erased by using UV (ultraviolet) light. Exposure to the UV light will erase all contents.
3. EEPROM (electrically erasable programmable read-only memory) - Similar to EPROM but its contents can be electrically erased and re-written without having to remove it from the computer.
4. Flash Memory - a modern type of EEPROM, it can be erased and re-written to electrically. It is much faster than EEPROM. It is ideal for electronic devices such as mobile phones and digital cameras.

Secondary Devices:

CD and DVD is Compact Disc (CD) and Digital Versatile Disc (DVD)

Types of DVDs:

DVDs can be divided into three main categories which are as follows:

1. DVD-ROM (Read-Only): These types of DVDs come with media already recorded on them, such as movie DVDs. As the name suggests, data on these discs cannot be erased or added, so these discs are known as read-only or non-writable DVDs.

2. DVD-R (Writable): It allows you to record or write information to the DVD. However, you can write information only once as it becomes a read-only DVD once it is full.

3. DVD-RW (Rewritable or Erasable): This type of disc can be erased, written, or recorded multiple times.

- DVD is short for digital versatile disc or digital video disc. It is a type of optical media used for storing optical data.
- Although it has the same size as a CD, its storage capacity is much more than a CD. So, it is widely used for storing and viewing movies

Computer networking:

refers to interconnected computing devices that can exchange data and share resources with each other.

- These networked devices use a system of rules, called communications protocols, to transmit information over physical or wireless technologies.

Difference b/w LAN MAN WAN		
LAN LOCAL AREA NETWORK	MAN METROPOLITAN AREA NETWORK	WAN WIDE AREA NETWORK
Use Building Office School , house	Multiple building , or in a city	Multiple city , country
Network Range 10m – 1000m	5km – 50km	1000000km
Example Ethernet , Wifi	Cable tv network	Internet

Network Standardization

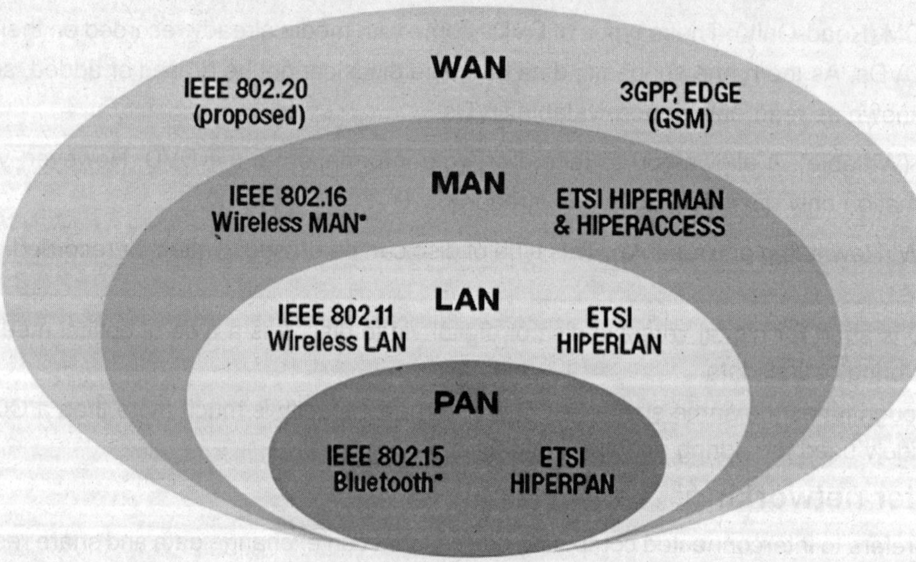

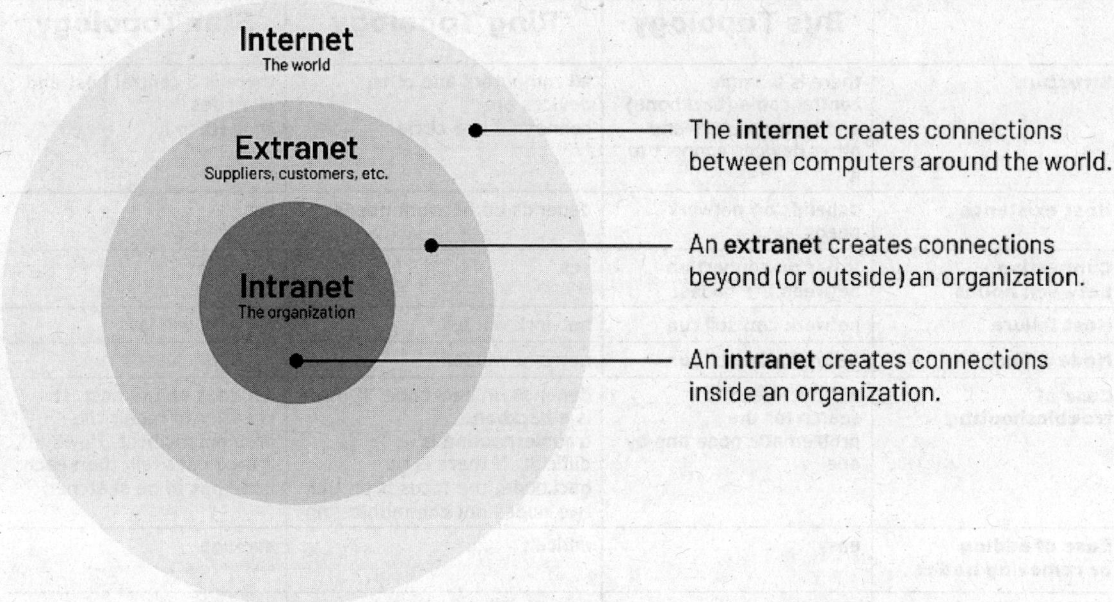
Internet
The world
Extranet
Suppliers, customers, etc.
Intranet
The organization
The **internet** creates connections between computers around the world.
An **extranet** creates connections beyond (or outside) an organization.
An **intranet** creates connections inside an organization.

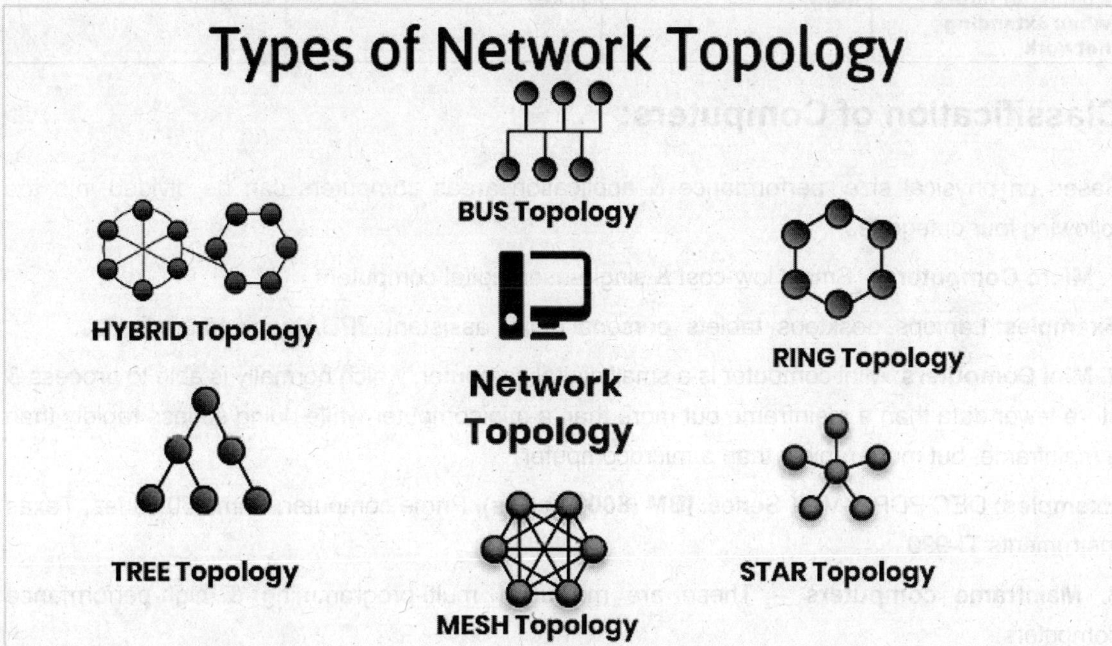
Types of Network Topology
BUS Topology
HYBRID Topology
RING Topology
Network Topology
TREE Topology
STAR Topology
MESH Topology

	Bus Topology	Ring Topology	Star Topology
Structure	there is a single central cable (backbone) and all computers and other devices connect to it	all computers and other devices are connected in a circle	there is a central host and all nodes connect to it
Host existence	depends on network needs	depends on network needs	yes
Connection between nodes	It has no connection between the nodes.	yes	no
Host failure	network can still run	network will fail	network will fail
Node failure	network can still run	network will fail	network can still run
Ease of troubleshooting	difficult. Need to search for the problematic node one by one	depends on backbone. If there is a backbone, troubleshooting is difficult. If there is no backbone, the focus is on the two nodes not communicating	depends on the host. It is easier to repair the problematic host. However, if the nodes fail, then each node has to be searched
Ease of adding or removing nodes	easy	difficult	average
Number of nodes when extending network	many	limited	limited

Classification of Computers:

Based on physical size, performance & application areas computers can be divided into the following four categories:

1. Micro Computers – Small, low-cost & single-user digital computers.

Examples: Laptops, desktops, tablets, personal digital assistants (PDA), and smartphones.

2. Mini Computers: Mini computer is a small digital computer, which normally is able to process & store fewer data than a mainframe but more than a minicomputer while doing so less rapidly than a mainframe, but more rapidly than a microcomputer.

Examples: DEC PDP & VAX Series, **IBM (8000 series),** Prime computer, Prime 50 series, Texas Instruments TI-990

3. Mainframe computers – These are multiuser, multi-programming & high-performance computers.

= Mainframe processes data at several million instructions per second (MIPS). More than 1,000 remoter work-stations can be accommodated by a typical mainframe computer.

Examples: **IBM'S E5000**, VAX 8000 & CDC 6600

4. Super Computer:

- They are the fastest and the most expensive machines
- The speed of a computer is generally measured in FLOPS (Floating Point Operation per Second)

- Any computer below one gigaflop/sec. is not considered a supercomputer.
- Its processing speed lies in the range of 400-10,000 MFLOPS.
- Summit or OLCF-4 is a super computer developed by IBM (International Business Machine Corporation) is the fastest super computer in the world.
- Pratyush is currently the fastest super computer in India.
- Super computer PARAM-8000 (made by the Centre Development of Advanced Computing (C-DAC) was launched on July 1, 1991 is considered India's first super computer.

COMPUTER GENERATIONS

GENERATION	HARDWARE COMPONENTS		CHARACTERISTICS	COMPUTERS
First Generation (1942-1959)		⊙ Vaccum Tubes	⊙ Machine Language ⊙ Huge Size ⊙ Highly Expensive ⊙ High Consumption of Electricity	⊙ ENIAC ⊙ UNIVAC ⊙ EDVAC ⊙ EDSAC ⊙ IBM-701
Second Generation (1959-1965)		⊙ Transistors ⊙ Magnetic Tapes	⊙ Batch processing, Multiprogramming OS ⊙ Expensive ⊙ FORTRAN, COBOL	⊙ IBM 7000 ⊙ CDC 1604 ⊙ ATLAS ⊙ NCR 304 ⊙ Honeywell 400
Third Generation (1965-1975)		⊙ Integrated Circuits	⊙ Remote processing, time-sharing, Multiprogramming OS ⊙ Faster, Compact & Cheaper ⊙ PASCAL PL/I, BASIC, ALGOL-68	⊙ IBM 360/370 ⊙ PDP 8/11 ⊙ CDC 6600
Fourth Generation (1975-1988)		⊙ VLSI Microprocessor circuits	⊙ Time-sharing, real-time networks, distributed, GUI OS ⊙ Faster, Compact & Affordable ⊙ C, C++, DBASE	⊙ DEC 10 ⊙ STAR 1000 ⊙ CRAY-1/II ⊙ Apple II ⊙ VAX 9000
Fifth Generation (1988-Present)		⊙ ULSI Microprocessor circuits	⊙ Parallel Processing & Artificial Intelligence technology ⊙ C and C++, Java, .Net	⊙ IBM ⊙ Pentium ⊙ Param

UNIT	ABBREVIATION	STORAGE
Bit	B	Binary Digit, Single 1 or 0
Nibble	-	4 bits
Byte/Octet	B	8 bits
Kilobyte	KB	1024 bytes
Megabyte	MB	1024 KB
Gigabyte	GB	1024 MB
Terabyte	TB	1024 GB
Petabyte	PB	1024 TB
Exabyte	EB	1024 PB
Zettabyte	ZB	1024 EB
Yottabyte	YB	1024 ZB

Quantities of bytes						
Common prefix				Binary prefix		
Name	Symbol	Decimal SI	Binary JEDEC	Name	Symbol	Binary IEC
kilobyte	KB/kB	10^3	2^{10}	kibibyte	KiB	2^{10}
megabyte	MB	10^6	2^{20}	mebibyte	MiB	2^{20}
gigabyte	GB	10^9	2^{30}	gibibyte	GiB	2^{30}
terabyte	TB	10^{12}	2^{40}	tebibyte	TiB	2^{40}
petabyte	PB	10^{15}	2^{50}	pebibyte	PiB	2^{50}
exabyte	EB	10^{18}	2^{60}	exbibyte	EiB	2^{60}
zettabyte	ZB	10^{21}	2^{70}	zebibyte	ZiB	2^{70}
yottabyte	YB	10^{24}	2^{80}	yobibyte	YiB	2^{80}

Measuring storage capacity

- **Bit**: A single binary digit representing a (0) zero or a 1.
- **Byte**: Made up of eight bits and represents the amount of space required to hold a single character.
- **Kilobyte (kb)**: Approximately 1000 bytes, or the equivalent of 1000 characters.
- **Megabyte (Mb)**: Approximately 1000 kb, or the equivalent of one million characters.
- **Gigabyte (Gb)**: Approximately 1000 Mb, or the equivalent of one billion characters.
- **Terabyte (TB)**: Approximately 1000 Gb.

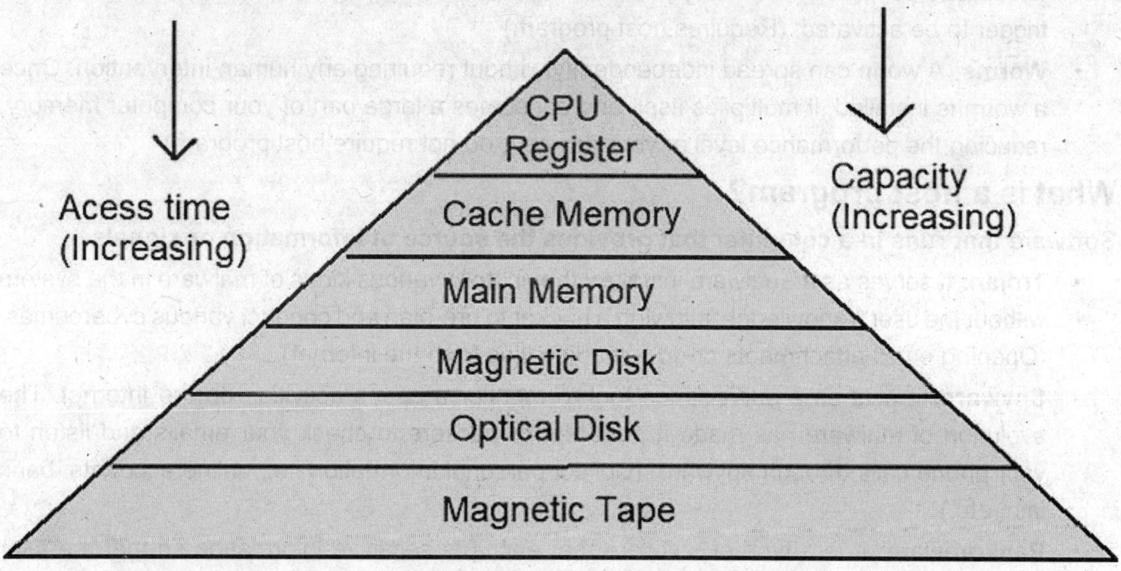

Fig:- Memory Hierarchy

Computer Registers

- Registers are a type of computer memory used to quickly accept, store, and transfer data and instructions that are being used immediately by the CPU.
- The registers used by the CPU are often termed as Processor registers.

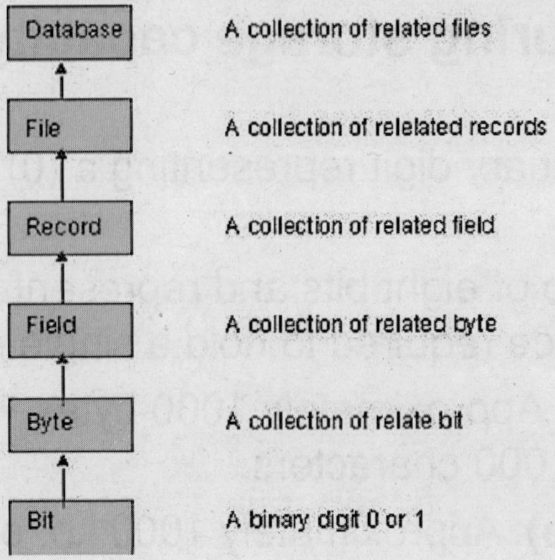

Malware

- **Malware** is a program designed to gain access to computer systems, normally for the benefit of some third party, without the user's permission. Malware includes computer viruses, worms, Trojan horses, ransomware, spyware, and other malicious programs.
- **Virus:** It is a replicating malware that is attached to a file. If you run that file, the virus will spread completely, infecting your computer and damaging your files. It usually needs a trigger to be activated. (Requires host program)
- **Worms:** A worm can spread independently without requiring any human intervention. Once a worm is installed, it multiplies itself and consumes a large part of your computer memory, reducing the performance level of your device. (do not require host program)

What is a host program?

Software that runs in a computer that provides the source of information or signals

- **Trojan:** It serves as a "malware installer" that installs various kinds of malware in the system without the user's knowledge, allowing a hacker to pre-plan and conduct various cybercrimes. (Opening email attachments or downloading files from the internet).
- **Spyware:** it acts as a surveillance tool to monitor a user's activities on the internet. The evolution of malware has made it possible for hackers to check your emails and listen to your phone calls through spyware. (Collect personal information i.e., online accounts, bank info, etc.)
- **Ransomware:** It is a type of software that encrypts sensitive information so that the user cannot access it. The hacker sends an unverified link to the user. As soon as the user clicks on the link, the hacker starts encrypting information that he might find valuable, which a mathematical key can only unlock. The hacker demands a ransom or financial aid, and as soon as he receives the amount, he unlocks the restricted data.
- (Block access to data unless a ransom is paid)
- Cookie: up to 4 kb files that recognize you and keep track of your info.

- Cookies are **files created by websites you visit**. They make your online experience easier by saving browsing information. With cookies, sites can keep you signed in, remember your site preferences, and give you locally relevant content.

Email

A way of sending electronic messages or data from one computer to another.

The parts of an E-mail address:

E-mail addresses often have three parts:

(1) The username

(2) The host or domain name

(3) The type of domain

Email Protocols: IMAP, POP3, SMTP, and HTTP E-mail Protocols are a set of rules that help the client to properly transmit the information to or from the mail server.

POP3 (Post Office Protocol 3): This is a simple, standardized protocol that allows users to access their mailboxes on the Internet and download messages to their computers. The simple design of POP3 allows casual email users who have a temporary Internet connection (dial-up access) to access emails. They can read their emails, draft new emails or reply to emails while they are offline, and can send these emails when they are back online.

IMAP (Internet Message Access Protocol): This is a standard protocol used for email transfer by users. Like POP3, it also supports both online and offline modes of email access. The email message is downloaded to the user's machine only when a specific request is made to read it. Users can download mail to their computers while keeping a copy on the server. The mails on the server are the primary copy and anything changed on the local machine is updated by what is on the server.

SMTP (Simple Mail Transfer Protocol): As the name suggests, SMTP is a simple, text-based protocol that works best when devices are interconnected to each other. However, the SMTP protocol can only be used to send emails. Unlike POP3 and IMAP protocols, SMTP does not provide the functionality to the users to retrieve emails from the server. This limits the use of SMTP to some extent. One of the main issues with SMTP is the lack of sender email authentication. SMTP lacks security features too and thus users get spam emails.

- **TCP/IP stands for Transmission Control Protocol/Internet Protocol.** TCP/IP is a set of standardized rules that allow computers to communicate on a network such as the internet.
- **An Internet Protocol address (IP address)** is a numerical label such as 192.0.2.1 that is connected to a computer network that uses the Internet Protocol for communication
- **A URL (Uniform Resource Locator)** is a unique identifier used to locate a resource on the Internet.

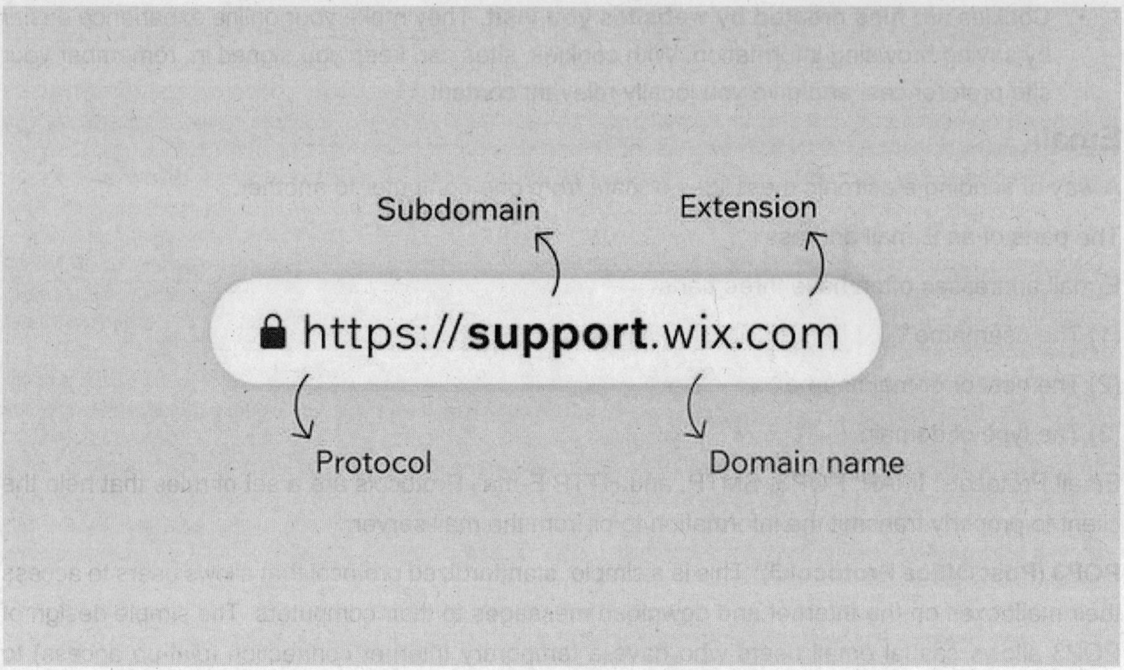

- Cc means carbon copy and Bcc means blind carbon copy.
- For emailing, you use Cc when you want to copy others publicly, and Bcc when you want to do it privately.
- Any recipients on the Bcc line of an email are not visible to others on the email
- BCC: It stands for Black Carbon Copy. It is utilised when we do not want one or more receivers to know that someone else was copied on the message.

Browser :

- An application used to access and view websites.
- Is a software application for accessing information on the world wide web.

Examples :

- Google Chrome
- Slimjet Browser
- Mozilla Firefox
- Maxthon
- Internet Explorer
- UC Browser
- Opera Web Browser
- Slim Browser
- Safari Web Browser
- Netscape Browser

Search Engine:

- It is a database or website which contains link to all web pages on the internet which help in search of information.

- Examples: Google, Bing, Yahoo, Ask.com etc.

Difference between Browser and Search Engine	
Browser	**Search Engine**
Programmed to browse a webpage	**to search for a webpage**
web browser can exist without a search engine	search engine needs a web browser to display its results
web browser is the basic element in accessing the Internet.	search engine is to simply search for keywords in a search engine's database.
you can't access any data without a web browser	**you can go to a certain website without the use of a search engine.**
a web browser is a software application that needs to be installed on a system	Search engines do not require any installation on any system and are openly accessible to anyone through the use of a web browser.
Access web pages and web sites	Searches and filters websites

- **Full forms**
- USB: Universal Serial Bus
- MOOC: Massive Open Online Course
- ALU: Arithmetic Logic Unit
- ASCII: American Standard Code for Information Interchange.
- NMEICT: National Mission on Education through ICT.

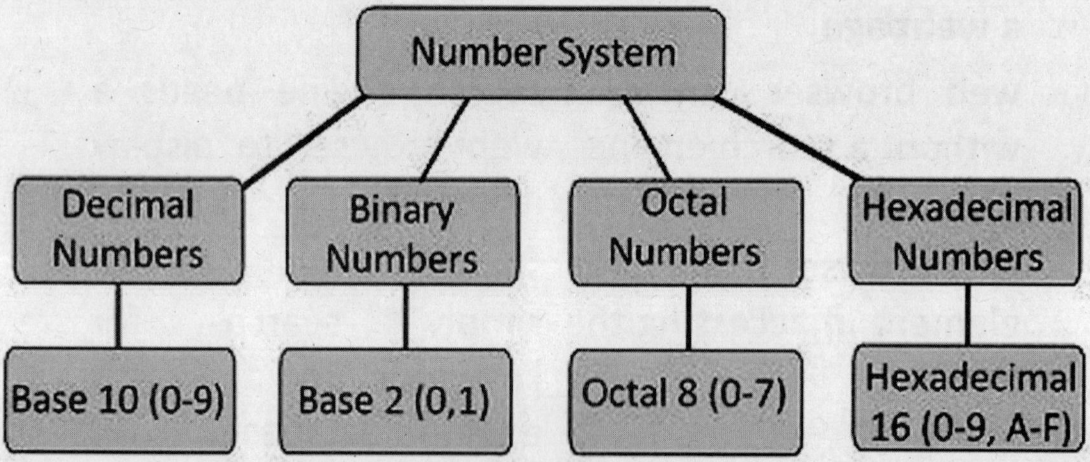

System	Base	Symbols	Used by humans?	Used in computers?
Binary	2	0, 1	No	Yes
Octal	8	0, 1, 2, 3, 4, 5, 6, 7	No	No/Yes
Decimal	10	0, 1, 2, 3, 4, 5, 6, 7, 8, 9	Yes	No
Hexa-decimal	16	0, 1, 2, 3, 4, 5, 6, 7, 8, 9 A, B, C, D, E, F	No	No/Yes

121_{10} ------ > Binary

Divisor	Number	Remainder
2	121	
2	60	1
2	30	0
2	15	0
2	7	1
2	3	1
2	1	1
	0	1

$121_{10} = 1111001_2$

1	0	1	0	1	0

$2^0 \times 0 = 1 \times 0 = 0$

$2^1 \times 1 = 2 \times 1 = 2$

$2^2 \times 0 = 4 \times 0 = 0$

$2^3 \times 1 = 8 \times 1 = 8$

$2^4 \times 0 = 16 \times 0 = 0$

$2^5 \times 1 = 32 \times 1 = 32$

Resultant decimal number= 0+2+0+8+0+32 = **42**

Octal to Decimal Conversion

Find the equivalent decimal number for octal 143_8

Place values	8^2	8^1	8^0
Octal	1	4	3
Conversion	$1x8^2$	$4x8^1$	$3x8^0$
Decimal	64	+ 32 +	3

99

Decimal Number: 33

8	33	1
8	4	4
	0	

remainder ↑

Octal Number: 41

Convert 114.7_{10} to binary:

2	114	
2	57	R 0
2	28	R 1
2	14	R 0
2	7	R 0
2	3	R 1
2	1	R 1
	0	R 1

↑ Read this way

0.7
x 2
(1).4
x 2
(0).8
x 2
(1).6
x 2
(1).2
x 2
(0).4
x 2
(0).8 ↓

Or we could combine the second and third techniques.

$$112_{10} = 1110010.1\overline{0110}..._2$$

$(10.625)_{10}$

Decimal to Binary

2	10	
2	5	0
2	2	1
2	1	0
	0	1

↑

0.625

0.625 x 2 = 1.250 ----- 1
0.250 x 2 = 0.500 ----- 0
0.500 x 2 = 1.0 -------- 1 ↓
0 x 2 end process

$$(16.625)_{10} = (1010.101)_2$$

CHAPTER 9

PEOPLE, DEVELOPMENT AND ENVIRONMENT

People, Development and Environment

1. Introduction and Basic terms

   a. **Environment:** Our surroundings are where living and non-living organisms interact.

   b. **Ecology:** Coined by **Ernst Haeckel** in 1866. (He is called as Father of Ecology). Ecology is the study of the habitat or territory or home of any organism. It could be simplified as the study of the ecosystem.

2. Two laws of Thermodynamics in Ecology:

   a. **First Law:** Law of conservation of energy. (Energy can neither be created nor destroyed, it can only be transferred.)

   b. **Second Law:** Increase in Entropy (lack of predictability i.e., you cannot predict natural disasters that may occur.)

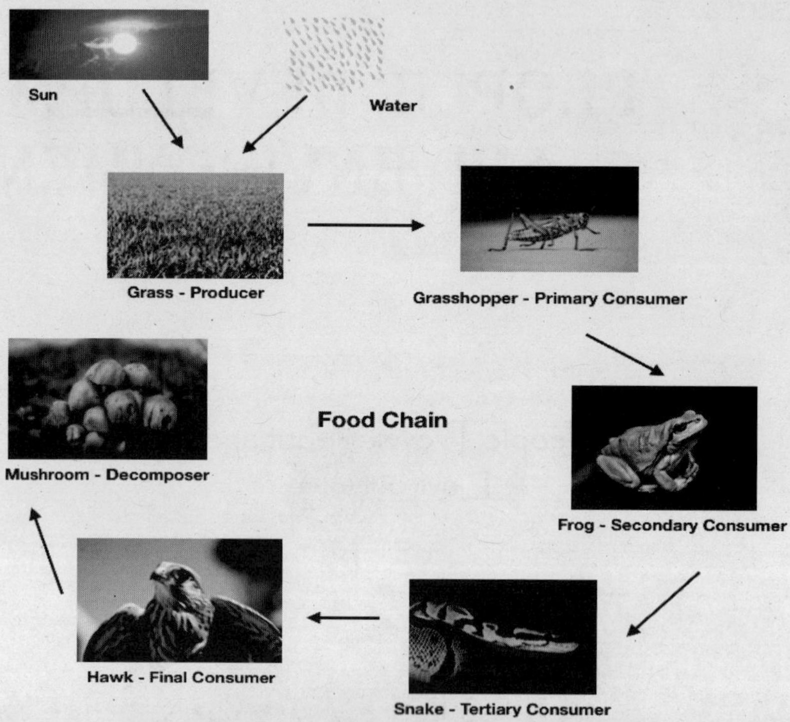

3. **Ecosystem:** Given by **Arthur Tansley** in 1935, Ecosystem tells us how organisms are linked through the food chain. It is a biological community of interacting organisms and their environment. It also tells the position of organisms in the food chain. In an ecosystem, the biological cycle of material is maintained by three groups i.e., producers, consumers, and decomposers.
4. **Producers:** Plants and some bacteria are capable of producing their own food with the process of photosynthesis. Animals obtain their energy and protein directly by grazing, feeding on producers is a **consumer. Decomposers** are the Fungi and bacteria that decompose the organic matter of producers and consumers into inorganic substances which can be reused by producers in the form of nutrients.
5. **Structure of Ecosystem:** Ecosystem can be divided into **Biotic and Abiotic.** Biotic components of the environment are humans, plants, animals, etc., and Abiotic components include soil, water, air, etc.

Components of Ecosystem

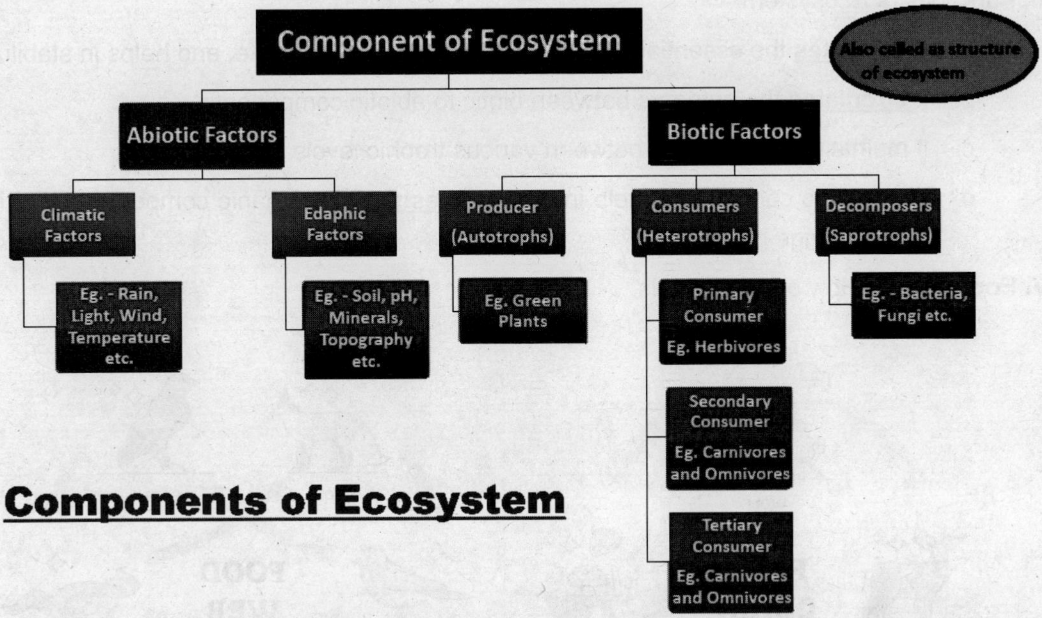

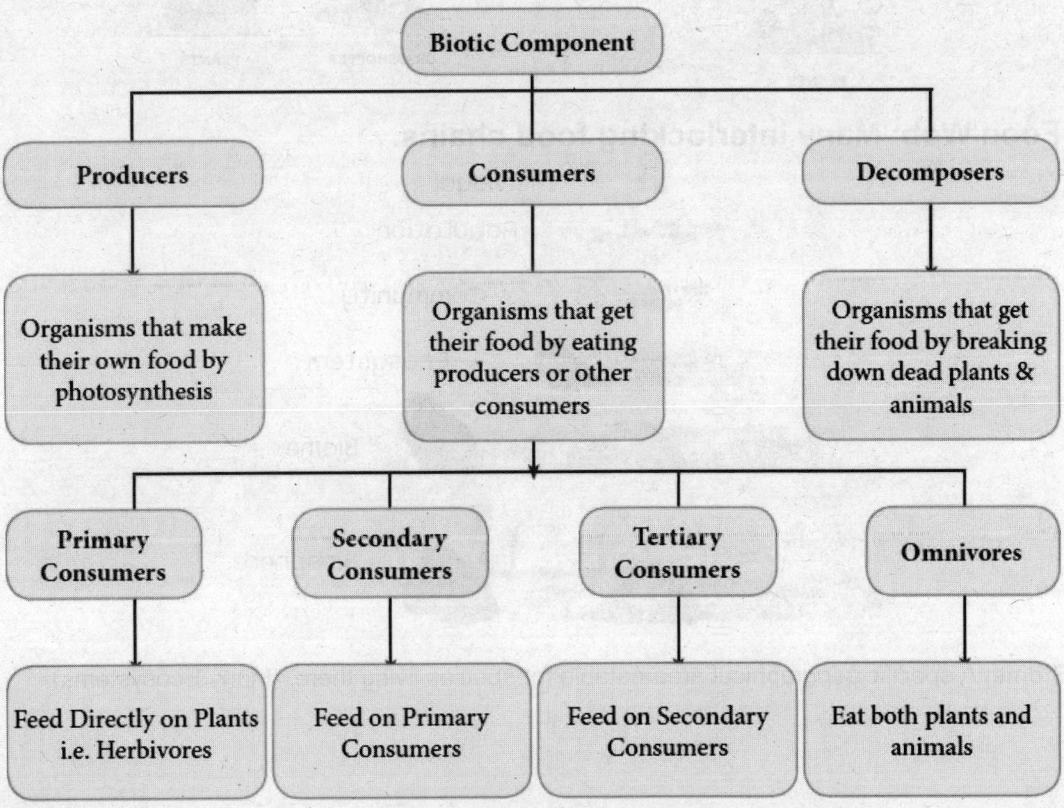

6. Functions of Ecosystem:

  a. It **regulates** the essential ecological processes, supports life, and helps in stabilizing.

  b. It **circulates** the nutrients between biotic to abiotic components.

  c. It maintains the **balance** between various trophic levels.

  d. The abiotic components help in the **synthesis** of the organic components that involve the exchange of energy.

7. Food Chain: How energy travels.

8. Food Web: Many interlocking food chains.

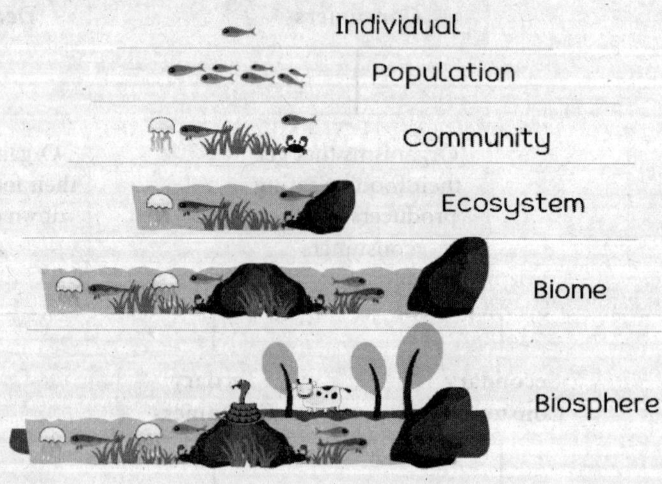

9. Biome: A specific geographical area notable for species living there. (Many Ecosystems).

10. Biosphere: Combination of LAH (Lithosphere, Atmosphere and Hydrosphere.)

Lithosphere (Land)	Hydrosphere (Water)	Atmosphere (Air)
Core	Surface	Troposphere
Mental	Vapour (in air)	Stratosphere
Crust	Underground (ground water)	Mesosphere
	Glaciers	Thermosphere
		Exosphere

11. **Ecological Pyramid:** - Ecological pyramid is a graphical presentation that shows the relationship between biomass or biological productivity and trophic levels. Pyramid o+by number shows the number of organisms from a producer at the bottom with the highest number to top carnivores. In the ecological pyramid by biomass, the amount of biomass at each trophic level is depicted. In the ecological pyramid by energy, only 10% of energy is transferred from one level to the other. This **10% energy law was given by Raymond Lindeman.**

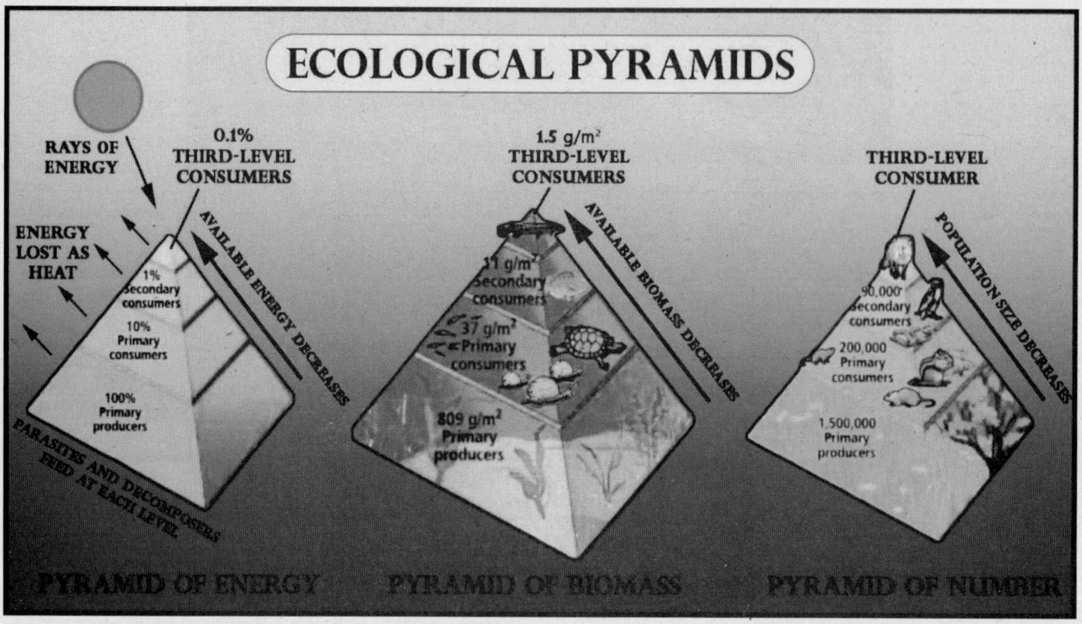

12. Types of Ecosystems:

(a) Terrestrial Ecosystem: This is a land-based community of organisms and interaction of biotic and abiotic components in the given area. The types can be classified on the basis of temperature range, precipitation received, soil type, and amount of light.

➢ **Forest Ecosystem:**

1. **Tropical Rain Forests**: Perennial rainfall, warm and good habitat, dense, moist soil but not rich.
2. **Temperate Deciduous Forest**: Big temperature changes, Hibernation, and migration, receive all four seasons, soil rich in minerals and nutrients as plants and trees are spaced.
3. **Taiga Forests**: Evergreen trees, cold weather-winter lasts up to 6 months with freezing temperatures, summers are short and warmer, thin layer of soil, and short growing season.

- **Desert Ecosystem**: Intense solar radiations, lashing winds, and low moisture, days are hot and nights are cold, persistently accelerating winds, high evaporation and transpiration, low flora, and fauna, organisms are xeric adaptive.

➢ **Grassland Ecosystem:**

1. **Tropical:** Close to the equator, between the two tropics, known as Savannas, usually heavy rainfall, South America, Africa, South Asia, and Australia are the regions. Grasses are tall (6-12 ft.), short deciduous trees, and support a wide variety of wildlife and crops.
2. **Temperate:** Amidst the temperate zones, Europe, North America, China, etc. are the regions, summers are warm and humid while winters are severely cold. Treeless with

short grass and grazing lands.

3. **Tundra**: Coldest and harshest, growing duration is 180 days, short summers.

(b) Aquatic Ecosystem

- **Ocean**: Saline, abundant, complex, range from low tidal to deep sea.
- **Lotic**: These are freshwater bodies like rivers, springs, etc., and oxygen level is high due to flowing water. Temperature also varies along the river. This habitat is influenced by the effect of continuously moving water, pollution, sediments, floods, and other human activities.
- **Lentic:** Standing or still water bodies like lakes, swamps, etc.
- **Estuarine:** It is a partially enclosed water body. Here salt water mixes with freshwater. High in CO_2, turbid water reduces the level of photosynthesis as it stops light to penetrate even 1 meter below.

Tropical Rainforest

Temperate Forest

Coniferous Forest (Taiga)

Tropical Grassland (Savannah)

Temperate Grassland

Mediterranean

Desert

Tundra

Mountain

"Facts to know"

- Environment Protection Act – 1986
- Term HOTSPOT was given by Norman Myris.
- There are 36 hotspots in the World and 4 hotspots in India i.e., Eastern Ghats, Western Ghats, Himalayas, Sundarbans.
- Biosphere Reserves are for preserving the original habitat of animals. Humans are its integral part.

- There are 18 biosphere reserves in India, out of which 11 are controlled by UNESCO.
- Biosphere has 3 zones:
    1. Transition Zone: Area of cooperation
    2. Buffer Zone: Where caretakers, doctors, and researchers reside in the biosphere reserve.
    3. Core Zone: Where animals reside and are preserved.
- Two strategies of preserving: In-situ (when original habitat is preserved) and Ex-situ (Artificial environment is made for preserving animals.)

Millennium Development Goals were started in the year 2000. Established by Millennium Summit – following the adoption of United Nation Millennium Declaration. These 8 goals need to be achieved by 2015.

INDIA'S PROGRESS TOWARDS ACHIEVING THE MILLENIUM DEVELOPMENT GOALS

KEY: SLOW MODERATE ON-TRACK

GOAL 1: ERADICATE EXTREME POVERTY AND HUNGER

1. Halve, between 1990 and 2015, proportion of population below national poverty line
2. Halve, between 1990 and 2015, proportion of people who suffer from hunger

GOAL 2: ACHIEVE UNIVERSAL PRIMARY EDUCATION

3. Ensure that by 2015 children everywhere, boys and girls alike, will be able to complete a full course of primary education

GOAL 3: PROMOTE GENDER EQUALITY AND EMPOWER WOMEN

4. Eliminate gender disparity in primary and secondary education, preferably by 2005, and in all levels of education no later than 2015

GOAL 4: REDUCE CHILD MORTALITY

5. Reduce by two-thirds, between 1990 and 2015, the under-five mortality rate

GOAL 5: IMPROVE MATERNAL HEALTH

6. Reduce by three quarters, between 1990 and 2015, the maternal mortality ratio

GOAL 6: COMBAT HIV/AIDS, MALARIA AND OTHER DISEASES

7. Have halted by 2015 and begun to reverse the spread of HIV/AIDS
8. Have halted by 2015 and begun to reverse the incidence of malaria and other major diseases

GOAL 7: ENSURE ENVIRONMENTAL SUSTAINABILITY

9. Integrate the principles of sustainable development into country policies and programmes and reverse the loss of environmental resources
10. Halve, by 2015, the proportion of people without sustainable access to safe drinking water and basic sanitation
11. By 2020, to have achieved, a significant improvement in the lives of at least 100 million slum dwellers

GOAL 8: DEVELOP A GLOBAL PARTNERSHIP FOR DEVELOPMENT

12. In cooperation with the private sector, make available the benefits of new technologies, especially information and communication

Sustainable Development Goals were adopted by UN in 2015, and targets are till 2030.

	Goal	Description	Target	Publication
1	No Poverty	End Poverty in all its forms everywhere.	7	48
2	Zero Hunger	End hunger, achieve food security, improved nutrition, and promote sustainable agriculture.	8	16
3	Good Health and Well-being	Ensure healthy lives and promote well-being for all at all ages.	13	46
4	Quality Education	Ensure Inclusive and equitable quality education and promote lifelong learning opportunities for all.	10	10
5	Gender Equality	Achieve gender equality and empower all women and girls.	9	45
6	Clean water and sanitation	Ensure availability and sustainable management of water and sanitation for all.	8	35

	Goal	Description	Target	Publication
7	Affordable and clean energy	Ensure access to affordable, reliable, sustainable, and modern energy for all.	5	44
8	Decent work and Economic growth	Promote sustained, inclusive, and sustainable economic growth, full and productive employment, and decent work for all.	12	47
9	Industry, Innovation, and Infrastructure	Build resilient infrastructure, promote inclusive and sustainable industrialization, and foster innovation.	8	16
10	Reduced Inequalities	Reduce inequality within and among countries.	10	13
11	Sustainable Cities and Communities	Make cities and human settlements inclusive, safe, resilient, and sustainable.	10	19
12	Responsible consumption and production and production	Ensure sustainable consumption and production patterns.	11	15
13	Climate Action	Take urgent action to combat climate change and its impacts.	5	35
14	Life below water	Conserve and sustainably use the oceans, seas, and marine resources for sustainable development.	10	40
15	Life on land	Protect, restore, and promote sustainable use of terrestrial ecosystems, sustainably manage forests, combat desertification, halt and reverse land degradation and halt biodiversity loss.	12	33
16	Peace, justice, and strong institutions	Promote peaceful and inclusive societies for sustainable development, provide access to justice for all, and build effective, accountable, and inclusive institutions at all levels.	12	13
17	Partnership for the goals	Strengthen the means of implementation and revitalize the Global Partnership for Sustainable Development.	19	73

Environmental Pollution:

Pollution is derived from Latin word "**Polluere**" which means to contaminate. Pollution is the effect of undesirable changes in our surroundings that have harmful effects on Earth. Pollution can be natural as well as manmade. Natural pollutants like volcanic ash and human-made could be runoff from factories or trash etc. Pollution deteriorates the quality of environment.

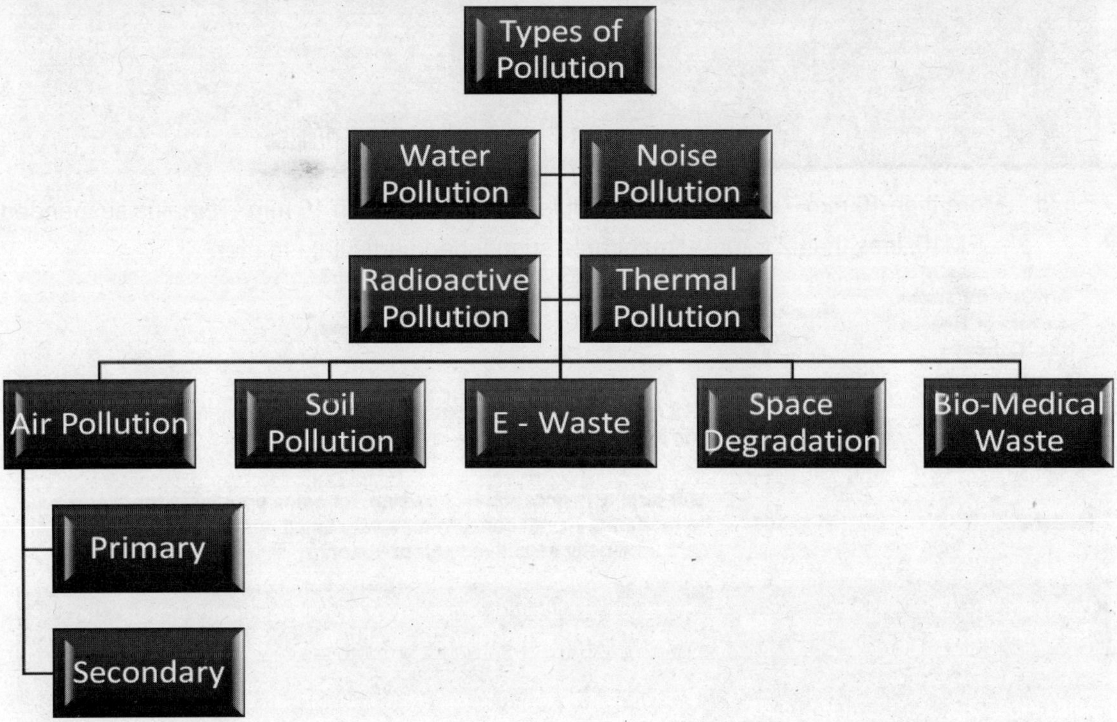

1. Air Pollution:

a. **Primary:** Pollution which is present directly in the atmosphere due to industrial or vehicular emission. E.g., Carbon dioxide, nitrous oxide, Sulphur oxide, greenhouse gases, etc.

b. **Secondary:** These pollutants are formed when atmospheric constituents act on primary pollutants. E.g., Photochemical Smog.

c. **Particulate Matter**: It is a complex mixture of solids and aerosols composed of small droplets of liquid, dry solid fragments, and solid cores with liquid coatings.

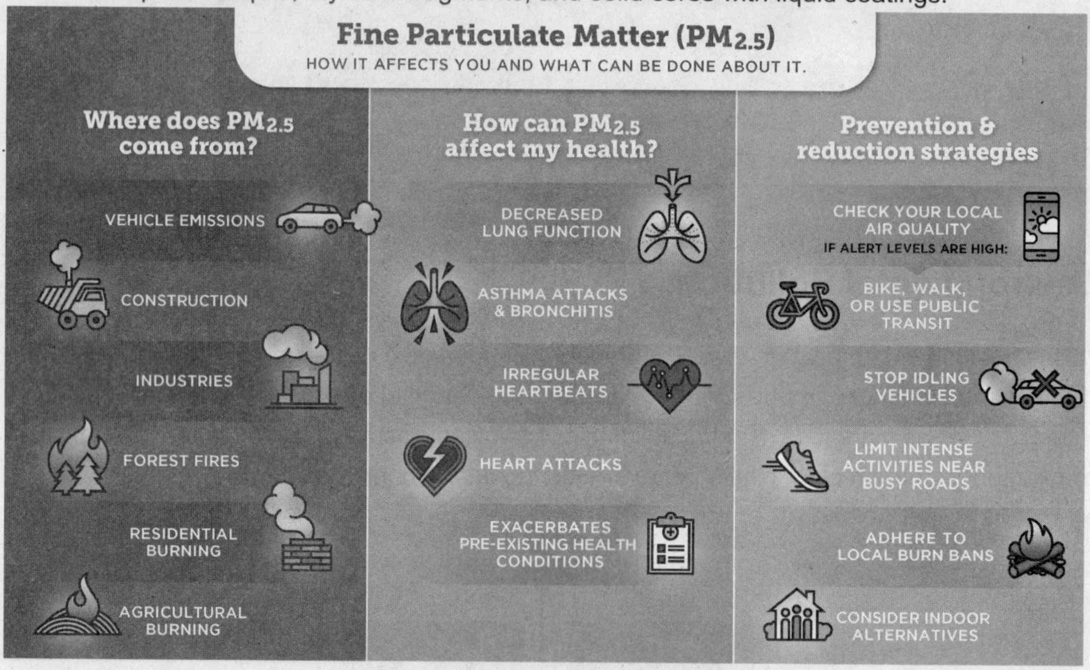

d. More than 10 mm – settle down in couple of days, less than 10 mm - remains suspended – PM10, less than 2.5 mm - respirable suspended particulate matter.

Air Quality Index Levels of Health Concern	Numerical Value	Meaning
Good	0 to 50	Air quality is considered satisfactory, and air pollution poses little or no risk.
Moderate	51 to 100	Air quality is acceptable; however, for some pollutants there may be a moderate health concern for a very small number of people who are unusually sensitive to air pollution.
Unhealthy for Sensitive Groups	101 to 150	Members of sensitive groups may experience health effects. The general public is not likely to be affected.
Unhealthy	151 to 200	Everyone may begin to experience health effects; members of sensitive groups may experience more serious health effects.
Very Unhealthy	201 to 300	Health alert: everyone may experience more serious health effects.
Hazardous	301 to 500	Health warnings of emergency conditions. The entire population is more likely to be affected.

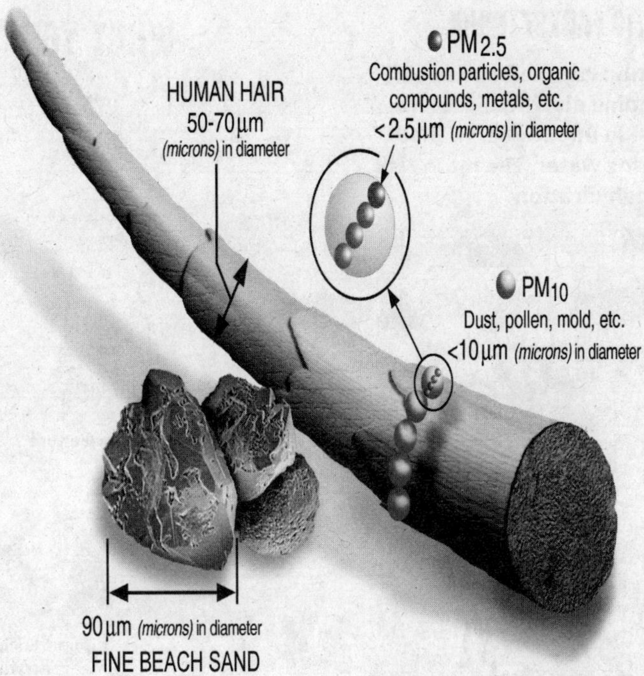

2. Water Pollution:

When a water becomes unfit for useful purposes by changing its quality or composition due to human activities directly or indirectly.

a. **Point Source of water pollution**

- **Industrial waste water:** The major reason for water pollution is variety of organic and inorganic waste from small and large industries.
- **Hot Water:** Industries such as thermal power plants and oil refineries use water as a coolant and dispose off hot water is water bodies disturbing the aquatic life and ecological balance of the river.

b. **Non-point Source of water pollution**

- **Municipal Wastewater:** Wastewater from domestic sources is sometimes discharged into the rivers, which is the major reason for pollution.
- **Surface runoff:** Agricultural run-offs affects the quality of ground water, when fertilizers and pesticides seeps into groundwater called as **leaching.**
- **Oil Spills:** It is an accidental discharge of petroleum in to oceans leading to pollution of marine ecosystem.

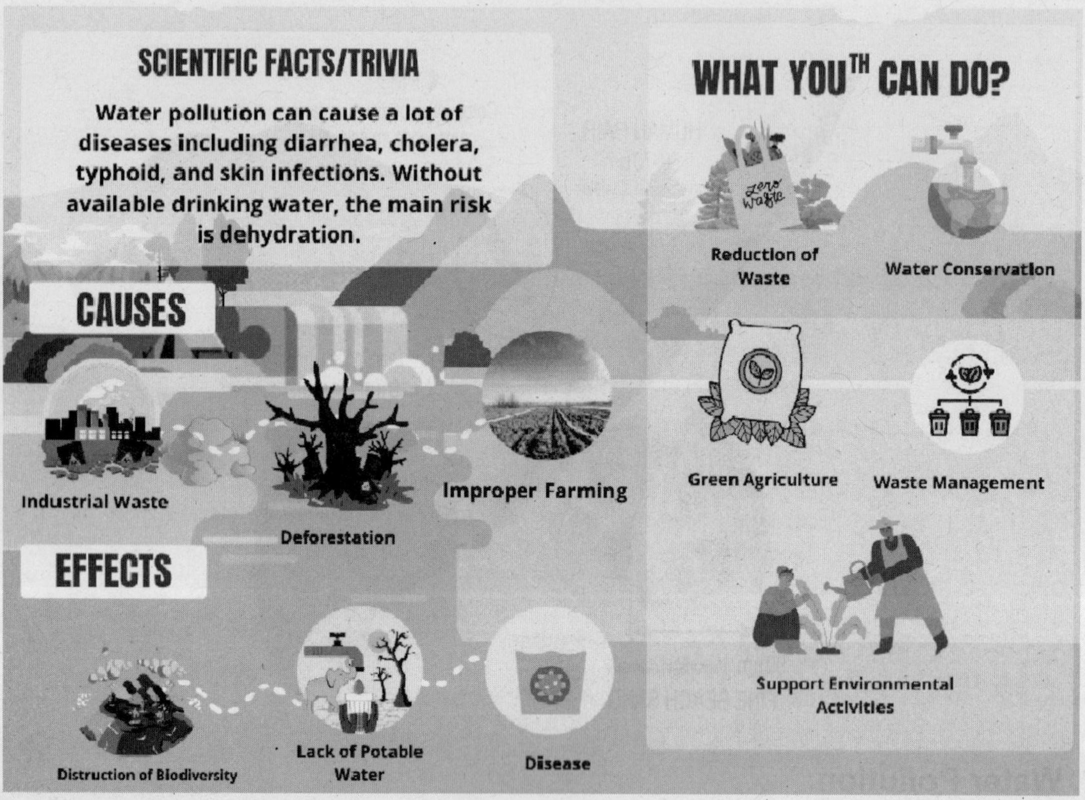

Causes of Water Pollution

a. Oxygen depleting waste

b. Urban run-off

c. Industrial wastes

d. Agricultural run-off

e. Leakages

f. Mining waste

g. Leachate from landfills

h. Inorganic Plant nutrients

i. Water soluble organic chemicals

j. Inadequately maintained septic tanks

k. Sediments of suspended matter

l. Water soluble radioactive isotopes Acid drainage into waters

m. Variety of organic chemicals

n. Oil spills

o. Hot water released

3. Noise Pollution:

According to the World Health Organization (WHO), noise pollution is defined as noise levels above 65 decibels (dB). However, it is important to note that noise can have harmful effects on human health when it exceeds 75 decibels (dB), and it can be considered painful at levels above 120

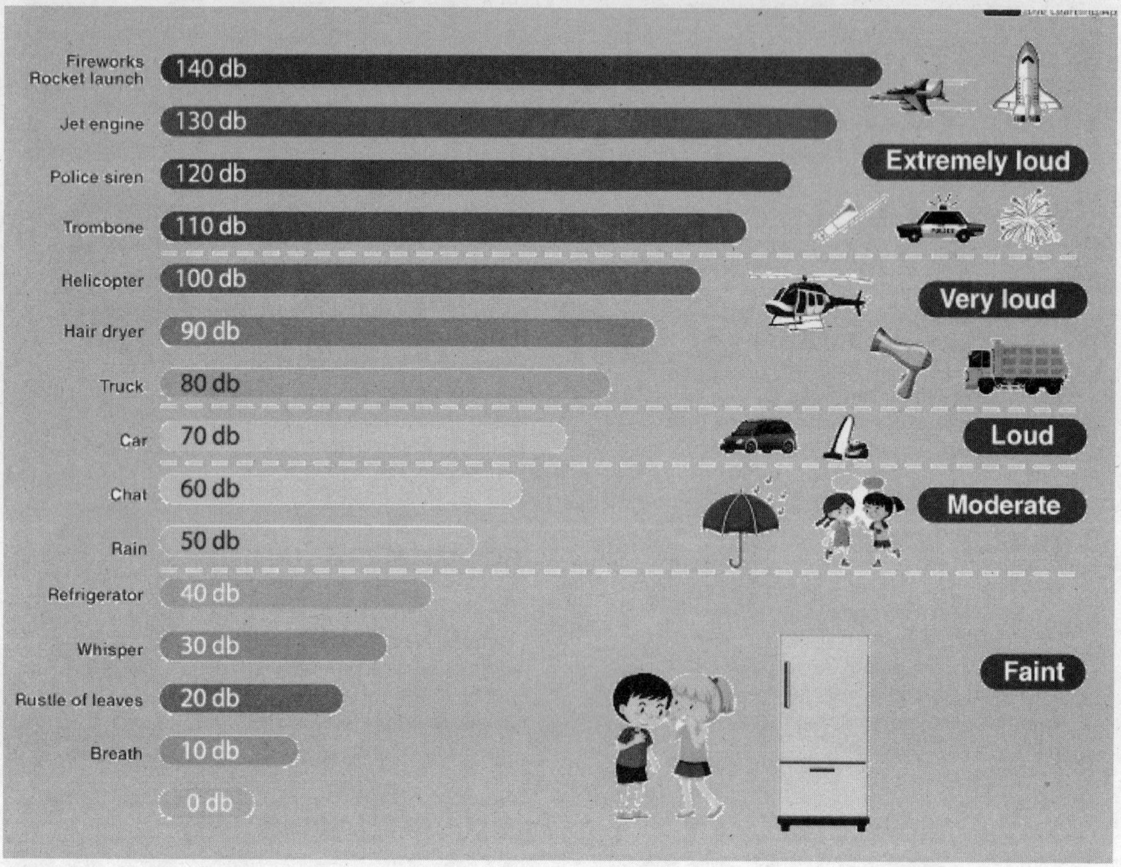

dB.

4. E-Waste:

When electronic or electrical equipment wastes are discarded can be termed as E-waste. It includes AC's, PCs, mobiles, fridges, remotes etc.

5. Space Degradation:

Due to presence of space debris or space junk present in the vicinity of earth. It can be both natural and artificial. They travel with the speed of 10km/sec. regarded as Vehicular Activity Hazard. Maneuvering and atmospheric drag are two methods of removing space debris which were discussed at conference in Berlin at 2013.

6. Bio-Medical Waste:

It is waste which is mainly from hospitals like bandages, human body parts, blood samples, syringe, expired medicines, etc. Part of this waste is infectious and hazardous. WHO in its 2007 meeting in Geneva defined the core principles for treatment of linked healthcare. The Blue Book, came in 1999 is the WHO hand book for safe management of waste. Second edition of this book came in 2014.

Conventions and International agreements particularly for Biomedical Waste Management:

a. Basel Convention on Hazardous Waste

b. Stockholm Convention (2006)

c. Minamata Convention on Mercury (2014)

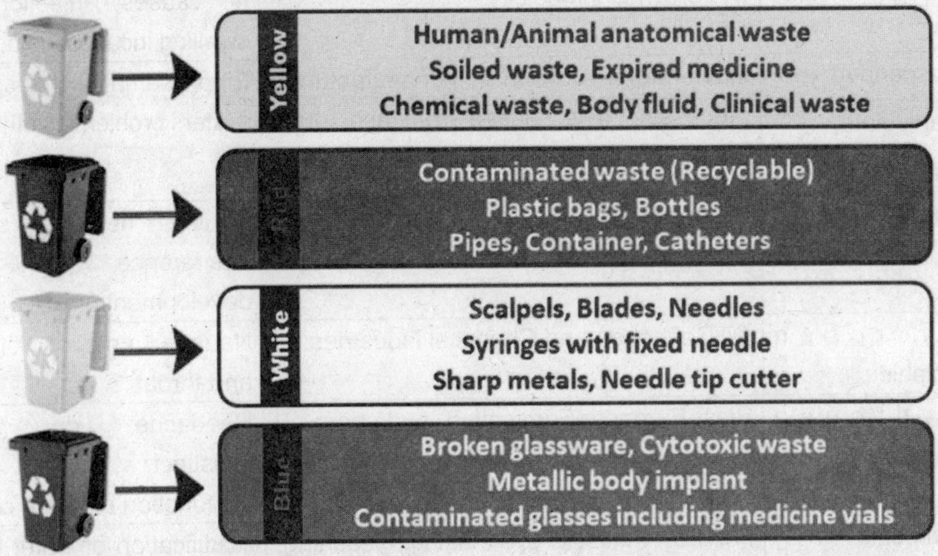

	Particular	Description	Effect
1	Carbon Dioxide (CO_2)	It is released when fossil fuels are burned. It is a greenhouse gas which results in warming up the earth's temperature. It is most abundantly present.	It results in global warming, melting of glaciers, climate change, sea level rise etc.
2	SMOG	It is a Smoke and Fog. It is of two types i.e., photochemical smog (which takes place due to reaction of NO_2 ¬with sunlight. It is also called as LOS Angeles or Delhi Smog.) and Sulphur Smog or London Smog which is caused due to SO_2 in the morning hours of winters.	Photochemical smog causes irritation in eyes and breathing problems. London Smog causes throat infection and breathing problems.
3	Ground Level Ozone (O_3)	It is bad ozone present in troposphere. Caused due to vehicular exhaust. (Carbon monoxide + hydrocarbon + nitrogen oxide = O_3)	It attacks lungs.
4	Sulphur Dioxide (SO_2)	It is released from thermal power plants and industries. It has nasty sharp smell. Sulphuric Acid (Acid Rain) = SO_2 + Rain	It causes severe respiratory problems.

5	Carbon Monoxide (CO)	It is due to incomplete combustion of fossil fuels, wood, cigarettes. It is toxic, colorless, tasteless and odorless.	It gets in blood and reduces the oxygen carrying capacity of the blood, breathing problems.
6	Nitrogen Dioxide (NO_2)	It is brownish in color	It causes infection and swelling in lungs, cold, flu etc.
7	Suspended Particulate Matter	Incinerators and manufacturing processes. It is caused from ash, dust, soot, aerosols, fumes, vapor etc.	Emphysema, respiratory system problems, asthma etc.
8	Lead	Leaded Petrol	Central nervous system, interference with development of RBC.
9	Hydrogen Sulphide	Oil Refineries and Chemical industries.	Nausea, irritation of eyes and throat.
10	Hydrogen Cyanide	Blast Furnace, Fumigation, and chemical industry.	Headache, dry throat, indistinct vision, and dysfunction of nerve cells.
11	Ammonia	Fertilizer industry, dye making, bleaching, and explosives.	Acidification of water bodies at high level.
12	Volatile Organic Compounds	They vaporize so easily at room temperature like ethanol etc	Smog formation
13	Green House Gases	Green house effect is the process that warms earth's surface. When heat is trapped in the atmosphere. Green house gases are CO2, methane, nitrous oxide, hydro floro carbon etc.	Global warming: natural causes volcano, forest fire etc., human causes industry, mining, deforestation. It results in heat waves, drought, heavy rain, heavy snow, species extinction etc.
14	CFCs (Cloro Floro Carbons)	Depletion of ozone layer was due to this artificial gas. It is non-toxic, non-flammable, alternate for ammonia.	CFC + Sunlight →Chlorine + Ozone → Ozone depletion.
15	Arsenic	Arsenic Soldering	Damage red blood cells, kidneys, and cause jaundice.

Some Important Concepts:

1. Rock Cycle: Conversion/transition of one rock to other. Chemical weathering **i.e.,** breaking or dissolving of rocks due to simultaneous rain and heat.

2. Types of rocks:

a. **Sedimentary Rocks**

b. Igneous Rocks

c. Metamorphic Rocks

3. Types of soil:

a. **Alluvial Soil:** Most fertile, formed with sedimentary rocks.

b. **Red Soil:** Rich in iron, formed with breaking of igneous rocks. Usually in low rain areas.

c. **Black Soil:** Regar Soil, it has water retention quality, ideal for cotton, rice, etc.

d. **Laterite Soil:** Clay + Red Soil, usually found in hot areas. It has low fertility.

4. Bio-Diversity: Variety of species of flora and fauna on terrain of earth.

5. Important Species

a. **Flagship Species:** These species are very important and they have danger of getting extinct. So, government makes schemes and make the brand ambassador of that scheme, hence giving protection.

b. **Endangered Species:** These are threatened species which are in danger of extinction if the current causal factors continue to operate.

c. **Vulnerable Species:** They have sufficient population today but they are depleting at a faster rate

d. **Rare Species:** The species which is very small and thinly distributed.

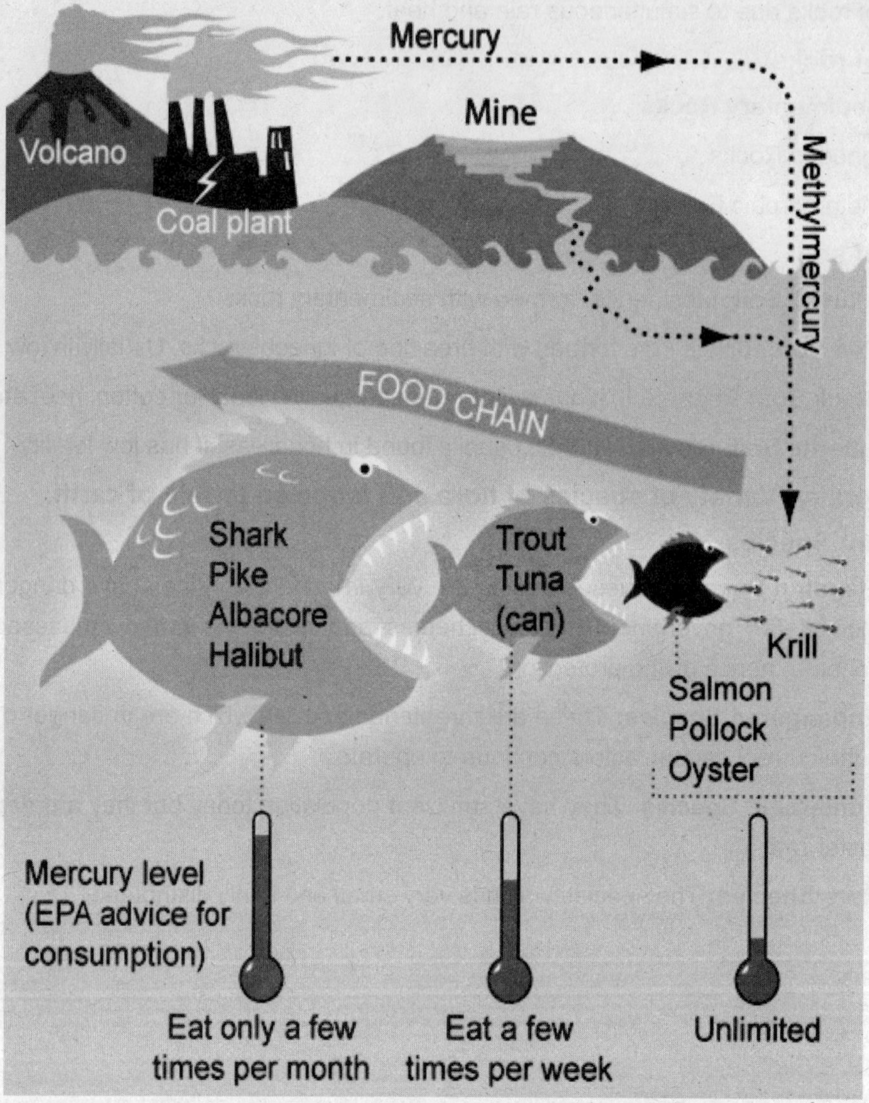

6. Bio-Magnification: Rise in the level of toxic chemical due to release from industrial sector. Minamata disease in Japan due to mercury in 1956. It affects central nervous system.

7. Natural Resources: Resources can be classified as renewable and non-renewable. Renewable resources or inexhaustible resources or modern resources include wind, hydro, solar, geothermal, biomass, etc. and non-renewable resources include coal, fossil fuels etc.

RENEWABLE ENERGY

MARKET SIZE

Installed Renewable Energy Capacity^ (in GW)

Note: ^ - includes wind, solar, bio power and small hydro

SECTOR COMPOSITION

Installed Capacity for Different RES (as of April 2022) (GW)

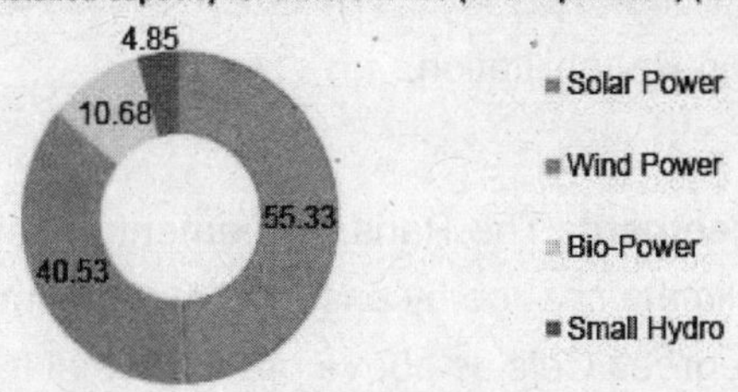

KEY TRENDS

Electricity Generation from RES (billion unit)

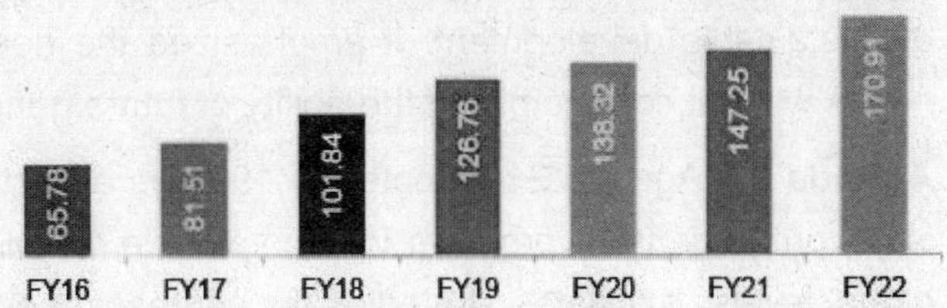

GOVERNMENT INITIATIVES

- **Green Energy Corridor**
- **Wind-Solar Hybrid Policy**
- **Solar Parks and Ultra Mega Solar Power Projects**

Natural Hazards:

a. **Geophysical** – Earthquake, landslide, tsunami, volcano.

b. **Climatological** – Temperature, drought, wildfires.

c. **Meteorological** – Cyclone, Storms.

d. **Hydrological** – Flood, snowfall.

e. **Biological** – Disease epidemic, plague.

f. **Hydro + Meteorological** – Snow avalanches, tropical cyclone.

Most frequent natural disaster is flood due to narrow river basins, deforestation, dam construction etc. Disaster management is done by Ministry of Home Affairs. It provides:

1. Timely warning system
2. Mock drill practices
3. Proper training system
4. Preventive measures to minimize risks
5. Provide Aid
6. Reconstruction
7. Relief camps
8. Rescue and Rehabilitation.

Conventions:

1. **Paris Agreement:** The Paris Agreement aims to enhance the global response to the threat of climate change by ensuring that the increase in global temperature is kept well below 2 degrees Celsius above pre-industrial levels. It was signed in 2015 as an action plan under the United Nations Framework Convention on Climate Change (UNFCCC).
2. **Brundtland Report:** The Brundtland Report, published in 1987, introduced the concept of sustainable development. It emphasized the need to meet present developmental needs without compromising the ability of future generations to meet their own needs.
3. **Agenda 21**: Agenda 21, adopted in 1992 as an action plan under the United Nations, is a comprehensive program for sustainable development at the local, national, and global levels. It outlines strategies for addressing environmental, social, and economic challenges while promoting sustainable practices.
4. **World Heritage Convention**: The World Heritage Convention, established in 1972, defines the types of natural and cultural sites that can be considered as World Heritage Sites under the United Nations Educational, Scientific and Cultural Organization (UNESCO). Its purpose is to preserve and protect these significant sites for future generations.
5. **Vienna Convention**: The Vienna Convention, signed in 1985, provides a framework for the protection of the ozone layer. It aims to control and reduce the production and consumption of substances that deplete the ozone layer, thus safeguarding the Earth's protective shield against harmful ultraviolet radiation.
6. **Ramsar Convention on Wetlands**: The Ramsar Convention, initiated in 1971, serves

as a framework for the conservation and wise use of wetlands and their resources. It aims to maintain the ecological character of wetlands, promote their sustainable utilization, and protect the important functions they provide.

7. **Convention on International Trade in Endangered Species (CITES)**: CITES, signed in 1973 and administered by the International Union for Conservation of Nature (IUCN), aims to protect endangered wild animals and plants from illegal trade. It regulates international trade in these species to ensure their survival and prevent their exploitation.

8. **Kyoto Protocol:** The Kyoto Protocol, adopted in 1997 under the UNFCCC, sets emission reduction targets for developed countries. It aims to combat climate change by committing nations to reduce greenhouse gas emissions and promote sustainable practices.

9. **Montreal Protocol**: The Montreal Protocol, agreed upon in 1987, is an international treaty aimed at protecting the ozone layer by phasing out the production and consumption of ozone-depleting substances. It has been successful in reducing the use of harmful substances like chlorofluorocarbons (CFCs).

10. **Minamata Convention**: The Minamata Convention, established in 2013 as a UN treaty, focuses on protecting human health and the environment from the adverse effects of mercury. It aims to minimize and control mercury emissions and promote safe handling of mercury-containing products and waste.

11. **Bonn Convention**: The Bonn Convention, initiated in 1979 under the United Nations Environment Programme (UNEP), aims to conserve migratory species of wild animals. It facilitates international cooperation to protect these species throughout their range and their habitats.

12. **UN Framework Convention on Climate Change (UNFCCC):** The UNFCCC, established in 1992 as an intergovernmental treaty, aims to stabilize greenhouse gas concentrations in the atmosphere. It provides a platform for international cooperation and negotiation to address climate change and its impacts.

13. **Basel Convention**: The Basel Convention, adopted in 1989, aims to reduce the movement of hazardous waste between countries. It promotes environmentally sound management and disposal of hazardous wastes and controls their transboundary movements to protect human health and the environment.

14. **Stockholm Convention on Persistent Organic Pollutants (POPs)**: The Stockholm Convention, adopted in 2001 in Stockholm, Sweden, aims to eliminate or restrict the production and use of persistent organic pollutants. These pollutants, such as certain pesticides and industrial chemicals, pose significant risks to human health and the environment.

15. **Benzene Convention**: The Benzene Convention, established in 1971, focuses on

preventing toxic substances derived from benzene. Benzene is a hazardous chemical commonly used in industries, and the convention aims to mitigate its adverse effects on human health and the environment.

16. **UN Convention on the Law of the Sea (UNCLOS)**: UNCLOS, adopted in 1982, establishes the rights and responsibilities of nations regarding the use of ocean water and marine resources. It provides guidelines for sustainable marine resource management, navigational rights, and the protection of the marine environment.
17. **Convention on Biological Diversity (CBD):** The CBD, adopted in 1992, aims to conserve biological diversity and promote the sustainable use of its components. It recognizes the importance of biodiversity for the well-being of humanity and promotes equitable sharing of benefits arising from the utilization of genetic resources.
18. **Convention to Combat Desertification:** The Convention to Combat Desertification, established in 1994 under the United Nations, addresses the issue of desertification and aims to mitigate the effects of drought. It encourages countries to implement national action programs to combat desertification and promote sustainable land management.
19. **Nagoya Protocol**: The Nagoya Protocol, adopted in 2010 as a supplementary agreement to the CBD, focuses on access to genetic resources and the fair and equitable sharing of benefits arising from their utilization. It aims to ensure that the utilization of genetic resources is done in a sustainable and mutually beneficial manner.
20. **Cartagena Protocol:** The Cartagena Protocol, established in 2000 as another supplementary agreement to the CBD, aims to protect biological diversity from the potential risks posed by living modified organisms (LMOs) or genetically modified organisms (GMOs). It establishes guidelines for the safe handling, transfer, and use of LMOs.
21. **Nairobi Declaration**: The Nairobi Declaration, agreed upon in 1985, is an agreement between parties to work together for the prosperity and sustainable development of the Western Indian Ocean region. It focuses on conserving marine and coastal resources, promoting sustainable fisheries, and addressing environmental challenges in the region.
22. **CITES Convention:** The CITES Convention, established in 1973, is a multilateral treaty resulting from a 1963 resolution by the International Union for Conservation of Nature (IUCN). It regulates international trade in endangered species of wild fauna and flora to ensure their conservation and sustainable use. Parties implement strict measures to control and monitor trade, protecting biodiversity and combating illegal wildlife trade. The IUCN provides support for its implementation.
23. **Geneva Protocol**: The Geneva Protocol, adopted in 1925, prohibits the use of chemical and biological weapons in warfare. It aims to protect civilians and combatants from the indiscriminate and inhumane effects of these weapons, establishing a norm against their use.

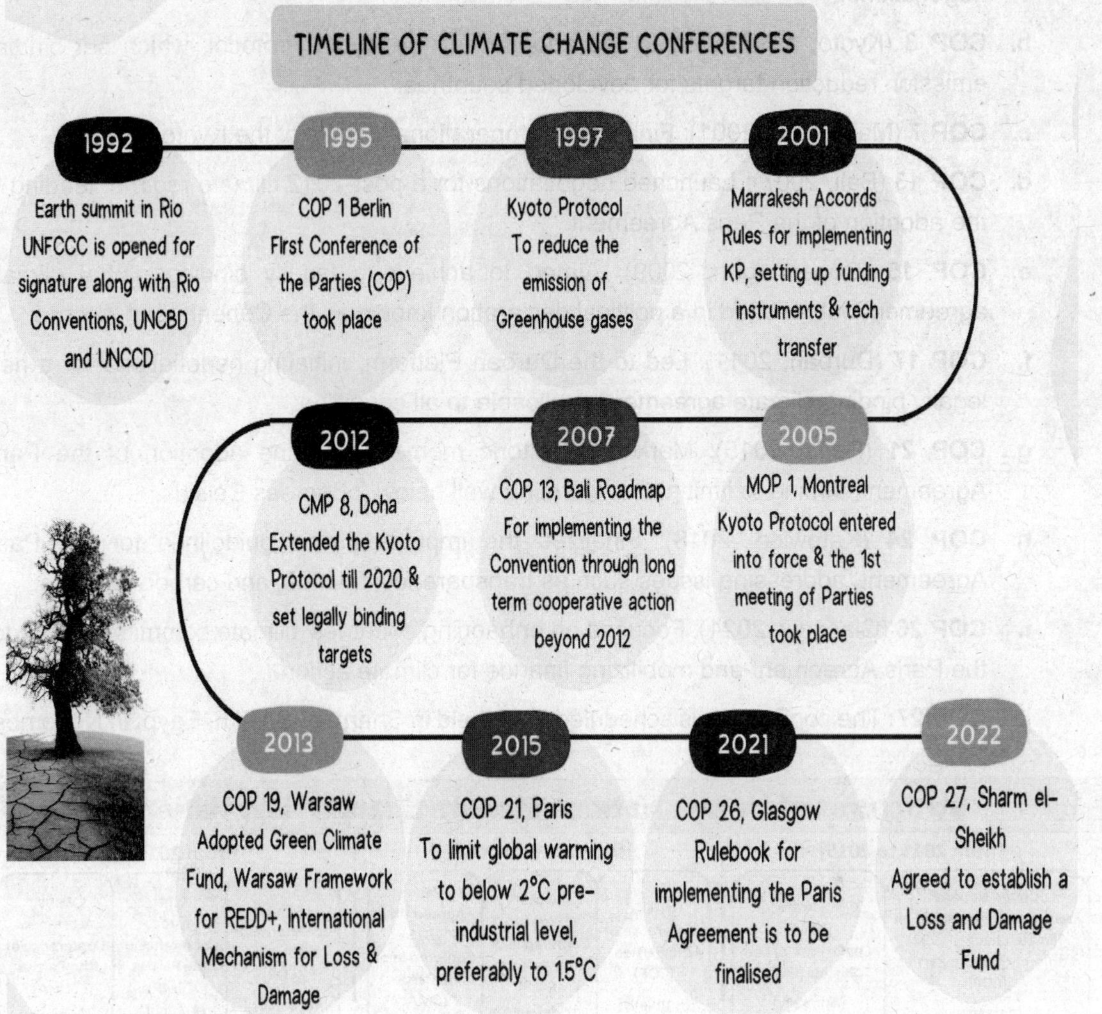

COPs: The Conference of the Parties (COP) is the decision-making body of the United Nations Framework Convention on Climate Change (UNFCCC).

a. COPs bring together representatives from countries worldwide to address climate change and make decisions on global climate policy.

b. COP meetings are held annually and serve as a platform for countries to discuss and negotiate actions related to climate change mitigation, adaptation, and finance.

c. COPs have resulted in significant international agreements that shape global climate action.

Important COPs:

a. **COP 1** (Berlin, 1995): Established the UNFCCC and laid the foundation for future climate negotiations.

b. **COP 3** (Kyoto, 1997): Led to the adoption of the Kyoto Protocol, which set binding emission reduction targets for developed countries.

c. **COP 7** (Marrakech, 2001): Finalized the operational details of the Kyoto Protocol.

d. **COP 13** (Bali, 2007): Launched negotiations for a post-2012 climate regime, leading to the adoption of the Paris Agreement.

e. **COP 15** (Copenhagen, 2009): Aimed to achieve a legally binding global climate agreement but resulted in a political declaration known as the Copenhagen Accord.

f. **COP 17** (Durban, 2011): Led to the Durban Platform, initiating negotiations for a new legally binding climate agreement applicable to all countries.

g. **COP 21** (Paris, 2015): Marked a historic moment with the adoption of the Paris Agreement, aiming to limit global warming well below 2 degrees Celsius.

h. **COP 24** (Katowice, 2018): Finalized the implementation guidelines for the Paris Agreement, addressing issues such as transparency, finance, and carbon markets.

i. **COP 26** (Glasgow, 2021): Focused on enhancing countries' climate commitments under the Paris Agreement and mobilizing finance for climate action.

j. **COP 27:** The conference is scheduled to be held in Sharm el-Sheikh, Egypt in November 2022.

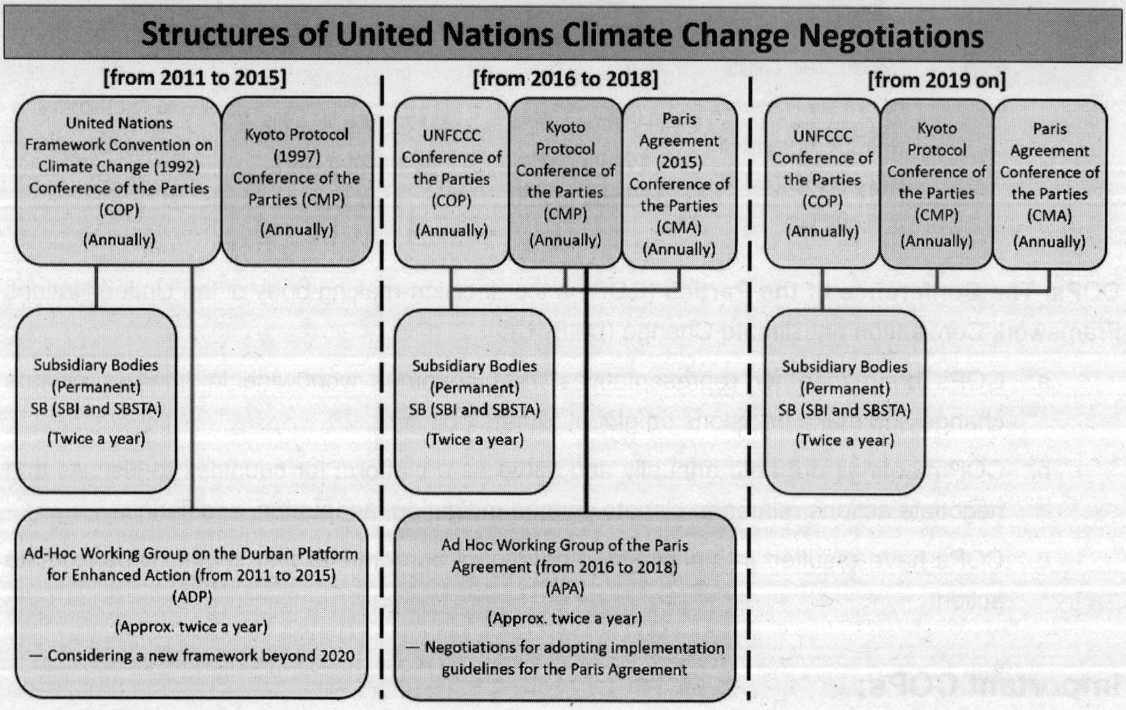

CHAPTER 10

HIGHER EDUCATION SYSTEM

Higher Education

Introduction of higher education in Ancient India:

1. Characteristics of ancient/conventional/traditional education:

- Oral and verbal teaching (students are passive)
- Concerned with self-realization or self-actualization.
- Knowledge of absolute (life after death/spirituality).
- Dependent on the "doctrine of action" or Karma.
- Gurukul Parampara.

2. Vedas:

This is concerned with Vedic education. Vedas contains 1028 hymns, 10580 verses, 10 mandals. Sanskrit was the medium of communication.

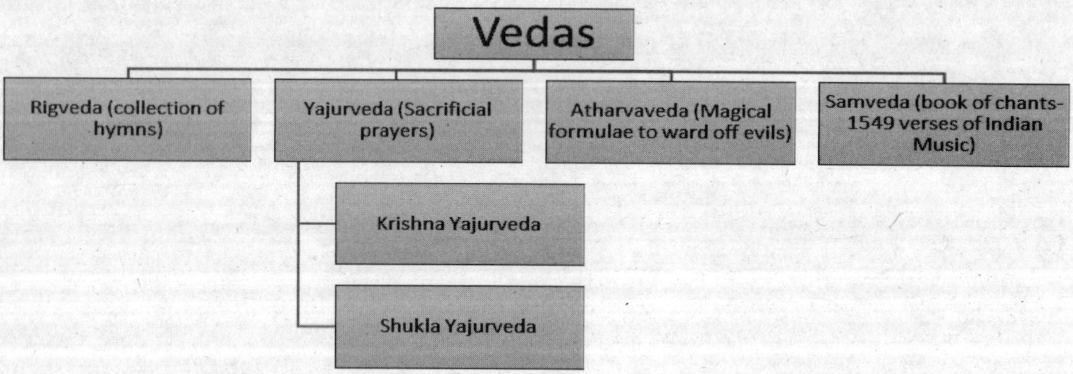

3. Stages of Vedic Education:

There are 3 stages of Vedic education.

- Shravana: To listen, memorize, and acquire and retain knowledge
- Manana: Analyse, derive a conclusion, and understand.
- Nididhyasana: Implication and application (applying truth to real life).

4. Education Centers in Ancient India:

- **Takshashila**: Takshashila, or Taxila, was an ancient city in present-day Pakistan. It was concerned with the religious teaching of Buddhism in a 6th century BCE. It taught medicine and military.

- **Vikramshila**: Situated in present-day Bihar, Vikramshila was another prestigious Buddhist learning center. It was established in the 8th century CE by King Dharmapala of the Pala dynasty.
- **Nalanda**: Located in present-day Bihar, India, Nalanda was a renowned Buddhist university and monastery. Founded in the 5th century CE, it flourished as a center of intellectual excellence for several centuries. Nalanda attracted students and scholars from around the world, offering a comprehensive curriculum covering subjects like philosophy, astronomy, logic, and linguistics. It had a massive library housing a vast collection of manuscripts.
- **Mithila University**: It was chief center for Nyaya and Logic by Gautam Rishi (12-15 century AD)

Evolution of Higher Education and Research in India

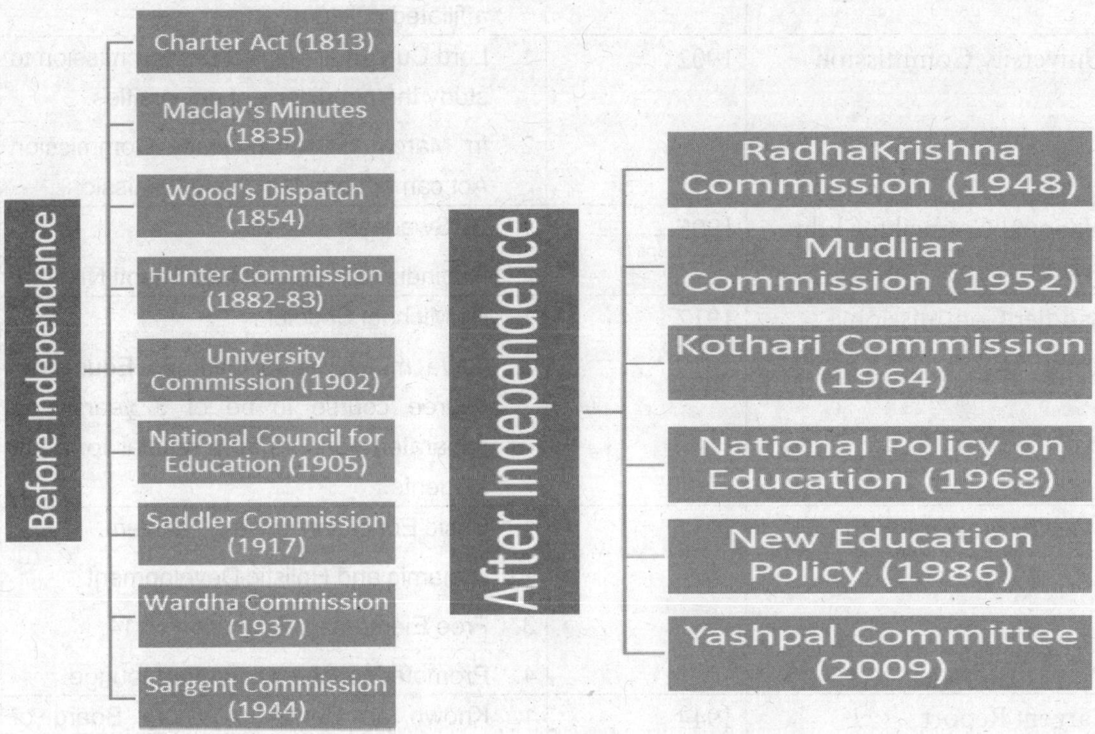

Commissions before Independence (1947)		
Name	**Date**	**Main Focus**
Charter Act	1813	1. To spread scientific knowledge

Maclay's Minutes	1835	1. English as a core language 2. Diffusion of English knowledge and culture 3. In-filtration theory (to educate upper class first)
Wood's Dispatch	1854	1. Magna Carta of English Education in India 2. Suggested setting up of 3 universities i.e., Bombay, Madras, and Calcutta in 1857. 3. Focused on women's education.
Hunter Commission	1882-83	1. Known as Indian Education Commission
		2. Suggested fragmentation of Education as Primary and Higher Education. 3. Suggested Universities to manage affiliated colleges.
University Commission	1902	1. Lord Curzon appointed the commission to study the conditions of universities. 2. In March 1904, University Commission Act came, based on this commission.
National Council for Education	1905	1. By Swadeshi 2. Rabindranath established Shanti Niketan.
Saddler Commission	1917	1. By Michael Saddler 2. Gave measures for Women Education, degree course to be of 3 years and separated honours from regular for merit students.
Wardha Commission	1937	1. Basic Education or Nayi Taaleem. 2. Dynamic and Holistic Development. 3. Free Elementary Education till 14. 4. Promoted teaching in mother tounge.
Sargent Report	1944	1. Known as Central Advisory Board of Education Report 2. Established UGC of England

Commissions Post Independence (After 1947)

Dr. RadhaKrishnan Committee	1948	1. Called as University Commission. 2. Focused on teacher's education and research. 3. It suggested integration of higher and secondary education by establishment of UGC in 1956 to promote and supervise higher education system. 4. Reorganization of HE by recruitment and curriculum design. 5. Rural education in backward areas.
		6. Medium of instruction to be regional language with one subject of national language and English.
Mudliar Commission	1952	1. Known as Secondary Education Commission. 2. Suggested establishment of multipurpose schools. 3. Recommended 3 year secondary and 4 year higher education system. 4. 3 Principles:- Training and leisure, variety and elasticity, integration and correlation.
Kothari Commission	1964	1. Education and National Development Report in 1966. 2. Focus on science, modernization, work experience, vocational education, women education, tribes, backward and schedule class. 3. Free books and study material. 4. 10+2+3 5. 3 language formula:- regional, national and foreign.
National Education Policy	1968	1. Compulsory free elementary education. 2. Mid-day meal. 3. Distance and Vocational education. 4. 6% of GDP on Education.

New Education Policy	1986	1. Focused on Quality Education. 2. Removal of disparity from the Educational System. 3. Operation Blackboard (1988). 4. In 1992 amendments were made.
Yashpal Committee	2009	1. Renovation and rejuvenation of HE in India. 2. Multi-disciplinary courses at graduation level. 3. Deemed to be universities to be converted in full-fledged universities. 4. 1:30 should be teacher pupil ratio.

New Education Policy 2020

The National Education Policy (NEP) 2020 is a comprehensive framework for the transformation of the education system in India. Here are a few major points about NEP 2020:

1. **Holistic Education**: NEP 2020 emphasizes a shift from rote learning to a holistic and multidisciplinary approach. It aims to promote critical thinking, creativity, and conceptual understanding among students.
2. **Early Childhood Education**: The policy recognizes the importance of early childhood education and aims to provide universal access to quality early childhood care and education for children aged 3 to 6 years.
3. **Flexible Board Exams**: NEP 2020 proposes a major reform in the board examination system. It promotes a modular approach where students can take exams in different subjects at different times during the academic year to reduce exam stress.
4. **Multilingualism**: The policy encourages the use of the mother tongue or local language as a medium of instruction in schools, along with the gradual introduction of other languages. This promotes multilingualism and preserves linguistic diversity.
5. **Technology Integration**: NEP 2020 recognizes the importance of technology in education and aims to integrate it effectively. It promotes the use of digital resources, e-learning platforms, and online teaching tools to enhance learning outcomes.
6. **Skill Development**: The policy focuses on integrating vocational education from an early stage to develop practical skills among students. It aims to bridge the gap between education and employment by providing hands-on training and internships.
7. **Teacher Training and Development**: NEP 2020 emphasizes the continuous professional development of teachers. It aims to improve the quality of teacher education programs, promote innovative teaching methods, and enhance the overall status and effectiveness of teachers.

8. **Higher Education Reforms**: The policy proposes several changes in the higher education system, including the establishment of multidisciplinary universities, increased focus on research and innovation, flexible curriculum choices, and the promotion of international collaborations.
9. **Equity and Inclusion**: NEP 2020 emphasizes the need for equal access to education for all, including children from disadvantaged backgrounds, socio-economically disadvantaged areas, and those with disabilities. It aims to bridge existing gaps and promote inclusive education.
10. **Regulatory Framework**: The policy proposes the establishment of a single, overarching regulatory body for the entire education sector, called the Higher Education Commission of India (HECI), to streamline and regulate all aspects of education.

Regulatory Framework of Higher Education in India

Policy Making	Regulation	Accreditation
Ministry of Education	University Grant Commission (UGC)	National Assessment and Accreditation Council (NAAC)
State Council for Higher Education (SCHE)	All India Council for Technical Education (AICTE)	National Board of Accreditation (NBA)
Association of Indian Universities	Medical Council of India (MCI), Bar Council of India (BCI), Pharmacy Council of India (PCI), Distance Education Bureau (DEB), National Council for Teachers Education (NCTE), Indian Council for Agricultural Research (ICAR), Indian Council for Medical Research (ICMR), Indian Council for Social Science Research (ICSSR), Council of Scientific and Industrial Research (CSIR)	
Central Advisory Board of Education (CABE)		

Functions performed by Central Government:

- Major policy framing and framework for HE

- UGC funding
- Legal status to universities under act of Parliament
- Declare the university as "Deemed to be".

University Grant Commission:

- Established under act of parliament in 1956 on recommendation of RadhaKrishnan Committee.
- Responsible for making rules and regulations for maintaining minimum standards.
- Serves as a link between government and Institutes.
- Release grants to colleges and universities.

NAAC:

- Autonomous UGC body established in 1994, headquarters at Bangalore.
- Checks quality of infrastructure, education, director, management, teaching-learning outcomes, research quality, and relevance and gives grades to institutes.
- Financial support for seminars, conferences, and major projects of innovation.
- Develop international linkages.

AICTE:

- It was established in 1945 in Delhi.
- It has 10 regional offices.
- It focuses on technical, practical, applied, and experimental areas.
- NBA is responsible for accrediting technical institutes.

Types of Universities:

1. On the basis of Establishment:

- Central Universities (Act of Parliament)
- State Universities (State Legislature)

2. On the basis of teaching style:

- Conventional/ Traditional
- Modern/ Electronic/ Digital/ Online

3. On the basis of Organizational Structure:

- Residential: Also called a Unitary University. No other branches are affiliated to this university. They have autonomy in decision-making.
- Affiliating: It affiliates colleges, acts as an examining body, and helps colleges in documentation or paper checking works.
- Both Residential and Affiliating: Dual mode universities. They provide both education and affiliation. Also called as Federal University.

4. Deemed to be University:

- It is the status given by Central Government to the institutes who performs exceptionally well.
- To obtain a status of deemed, an institute has to provide multidisciplinary courses, which enhance employment opportunities.

- They are given autonomy to take decision regarding curriculum, exams, finances etc.

5. Open University/Distance Education/Online Learning:

- Doorstep education, a flexible education system in a virtual environment.
- Objective is the universalization of education, liquidating illiteracy, democraticising education.
- IGNOU (Indra Gandhi National Open University) is the Central Open University in Delhi opened in 1985.
- IGNOU Channels: Gyandarshan for Socials Sciences and Eklavya for Technical Education.
- State Open Universities (currently 13).
- B.R. Ambedkar in 1982 opened first open university in Andhra Pradesh.

Academic Administration of Universities:

Chancellor

Vice Chancellor

Dean (Significant authority in academic unit)

HOD (Head of Department)

Academic Council (Maintain standard of instructions, education and examination. They advice executive council)

Board Of Studies (Set course or papers)

Syndicate or Executive Council (Handles day to day administration of university)

Board of Management (Perform statutory function and appoints and approve teachers.)

Registrar (Keeps records)

Policies and Governance

1. MOOC: Massive Open Online Course (2006). Taught by prestigious Indian and foreign institutes on platforms like MIT, Coursera, Swayam, OCW etc.

a. **SWAYAM:** Study Web of Active Learning For Young Aspiring Minds

b. **SWAYAMPRABHA:** 32 DTH Channels that are telecasted by G-SAT 15 satellite.

c. **EDU-SAT:** Launched by ISRO for Education on 20 September 2004.

2. NAEP: National Adult Education Programme on 2nd October 1978 to eradicate illiteracy among adults between 15-35.

3. NMEICT: National Mission on Education through ICT by MOE to provide quality education content to willing learners via internet.

4. E-Pathshala: Jointly started by MHRD and NCERT which provide wide range of educational e-resources. It is a digital library.

5. RUSA: Rashtriya Uchattar Siksha Abhiyaan, National higher education mission by MHRD(now MOE) in 2013. Central scheme that aimed at providing funds to HE institutes. It covered 316 state universities and 13024 colleges.

6. NPTEL: National Programme on Technology Based Learning. It is an initiative by seven IITs (Delhi, Guwahati, Kanpur, Kharagpur, Bombay, Madras and Roorkee) and IISc for creating course contents in engineering and science.

Digital Initiatives

1. **(Massive Open Online Course): MOOCs** are online courses that are open to a large number of participants. They are offered by various educational institutions and platforms, allowing learners to access high-quality educational content from anywhere and at their own pace.
2. **SWAYAM (Study Webs of Active-Learning for Young Aspiring Minds) - 2017:** SWAYAM is an online platform in India that provides free courses from renowned institutions. It offers a wide range of subjects and levels, including school education, undergraduate and postgraduate courses, and skill-based programs.
3. **SWAYAM Prabha – 2017:** SWAYAM Prabha is a group of 32 direct-to-home (DTH) educational channels in India that broadcast educational content in various disciplines. The channels feature lectures and courses from professors and experts, offering students access to quality educational material.
4. **National Digital Library (NDL) - 2015:** The National Digital Library of India is a digital repository that provides a wide range of educational resources, including textbooks, audio and video lectures, journals, and other learning materials. It aims to facilitate universal access to knowledge and support the learning needs of students and teachers.
5. **National Academic Depository (NAD) - 2017:** NAD is a centralized digital repository of academic certificates, diplomas, degrees, and other academic documents. It provides an

online platform for students, educational institutions, and employers to store, verify, and access academic records securely.

6. **e-ShodhSindhu - 2015:** e-ShodhSindhu is an initiative in India that provides access to electronic resources, including scholarly journals, e-books, databases, and research papers, to academic institutions. It aims to enhance research capabilities and promote collaboration among researchers and students.
7. **Virtual Labs – 2010:** Virtual Labs are online platforms that simulate laboratory experiments and provide a virtual environment for students to conduct scientific experiments and learn practical aspects of various subjects. It helps overcome limitations of physical laboratory infrastructure and enhances understanding of scientific concepts.
8. **e-Yantra - 2009:** e-Yantra is an initiative in India that promotes robotics education in engineering colleges. It offers online courses, robotics kits, and training to students and faculty members, fostering innovation and practical skills in the field of robotics.
9. **Campus Connectivity:** Campus Connectivity initiatives focus on improving internet connectivity and network infrastructure in educational institutions. It ensures seamless access to digital resources, online learning platforms, and facilitates communication and collaboration among students and faculty.
10. **Talk to a Teacher:** Talk to a Teacher is a platform that provides students with the opportunity to interact with experienced teachers through phone calls or online platforms. It offers guidance, counseling, and clarifications on academic subjects and career-related queries.
11. **e-Acharya**: e-Acharya is an online platform that offers postgraduate-level courses in various disciplines, enabling professionals and individuals to pursue higher education remotely.
12. **e-Kalpa**: e-Kalpa is a digital initiative that provides access to visual and audiovisual content related to various subjects, including arts, sciences, and humanities. It aims to enhance learning experiences through multimedia resources.
13. **e-Vidwan:** e-Vidwan is an online database that showcases profiles and research information of academic experts and faculty members from various disciplines in India. It helps researchers, institutions, and policymakers identify and collaborate with experts in specific domains.
14. **NIRF (National Institutional Ranking Framework) - 2015:** NIRF is a framework established by the Government of India to rank higher education institutions based on various parameters such as teaching, research, and outreach activities. It provides a comprehensive rankIng system to help students and stakeholders make informed decisions.
15. **GIAN (Global Initiative of Academic Networks) - 2015:** GIAN is an initiative in India that invites reputed international faculty to teach short-term courses and conduct research collaborations in Indian higher education institutions. It aims to promote knowledge and expertise exchange between Indian and international academia.
16. **RUSA (Rashtriya Uchchatar Shiksha Abhiyan)** - 2013: RUSA is a centrally sponsored

scheme in India that aims to improve the quality of higher education. It provides funding and support to states and institutions for various initiatives, including infrastructure development, faculty improvement, research and innovation, and equity initiatives.